Success leaves clues. Clint Schumacher is a man full of wisdom and integrity, and this book is proof. Clint takes decades of experience and distills it into a handful of actionable steps that the super-resilient use to bounce back from hardship. *Second Wind* is a powerful read for those working through an obstacle in their life and a practical guide for teaching people how to be resilient, written by a man who lives out what he teaches.

—**James Leath**, Mental Performance Coach, Chicago Bulls; Head of Leadership Development, IMG Academy; Founder, Unleash the Athlete

As coaches, two of the most important things we can teach our athletes are mental toughness and overcoming adversity. Clint Schumacher brings experience from two highly competitive arenas—high stakes litigation in the courtroom and Texas high school football—and shares insights on developing resilience in ourselves and those we coach or mentor. The lessons from this book are essential for those working with high school athletes.

—**Randy Jackson**, Head Football Coach at North Forney High School and Author of *Culture Defeats Strategy* and *Culture Defeats Strategy 2*

As parents, an important lesson to teach to and model for our children is what it takes to overcome adversity. In *Second Wind*, Clint Schumacher unpacks some of the key components of resiliency through a collection of fun and informative stories. This is a great read for any parent who wants to be intentional in raising resilient kids.

—**Cynthia Yanof**, Host of *Pardon the Mess* of the Christian Parenting Podcast Network

As lawyers—or lawyers-in-training—an essential part of a fulfilling career is being able to recover from and even learn from setbacks. In *Second Wind*, Clint Schumacher shares some of the lessons learned over his unique career. Using parables, stories, and experiences from his own life, Clint shows how it is possible to embrace the difficult parts of life and come through the other side even better. This is a great book for young professionals, or for those mentoring young professionals, who value the way that overcoming obstacles can accelerate growth. I recommend it, highly.

—**Robert Thomas**, Visiting Professor at William & Mary Law School, and Editor of inversecondemnation.com.

Second Wind

Decisions the Resilient Make to Overcome Adversity

J. Clint Schumacher

Published by Author Academy Elite
PO Box 43, Powell, OH 43065
www.AuthorAcademyElite.com

Identifiers:
LCCN: 2021901578
ISBN: 978-1-64746-702-9 (paperback)
ISBN: 978-1-64746-703-6 (hardback)
ISBN: 978-1-64746-704-3 (ebook)

Available in paperback, hardback, e-book, and audiobook

All Scripture quotations, unless otherwise indicated, are taken from the Holy Bible, New International Version®, NIV®. Copyright © 1973, 1978, 1984 by Biblica, Inc.™ Used by permission of Zondervan. All rights reserved worldwide.

Dedication

To my wife and sons, my parents, my brother and sister-in-law, my law partners, and my fellow coaches.

Thanks for all that you have taught me.

TABLE OF CONTENTS

PREFACE

Ideas can come from unexpected places. My study of resiliency was birthed on the sideline during a youth football game. Our team had a successful season, and we were playing for the league championship. This game, however, was not going well. We got behind early and the downward spiral began. As they fell behind, the players' eyes widened. Then, anxiety set in. As it became obvious late in the game that we were likely to lose, some players tapped out.

As I walked off the field, I was frustrated at the kids. How could they show so little fight? Why were they not able to bounce back from the early adversity and perform?

In the days that followed, however, it became clear to me that the failure was mine. As their head coach, I had not taught them what to do when things did not go our way early in a game. I had not talked to them about bouncing back from difficulty. They had not trailed in a football game in two years, so they were navigating—in real time—how to be resilient in the face of adversity. This was a hole in my coaching. I had left them unprepared.

So, I started studying resilience. What is it? How have people incorporated it into their lives? Can you learn it? Can you teach it? I began to take notice of people who bounced back from difficult circumstances. I observed what they did. I read about them. I talked to them.

I deconstructed times of adversity in my own life. Where did I succeed? Where did I fail? What did I learn? What could I take back to these kids and try to teach the next season?

This book captures what I learned and what I began to teach. There are key decisions that compel us from adversity to overcoming. The lessons I learned were for me. They were for my children. They were for the athletes I get to coach. Sometimes, they were even for my professional clients. I hope and have prayed that there is something in here for you. You are not alone on your journey and there is a second wind inside you waiting to be released.

INTRODUCTION

"We can't keep going through this." The barely audible words came from a raw place. My wife was in the passenger seat next to me staring blankly out the window. A tear stain still streaked her cheek. We were returning home with bad news yet again. For five years, we had been trying to grow our family without success. One failed attempt followed another. Even when a glimmer of hope arrived, something snuffed it out. Then, tears and a long car ride home would follow. "We can't keep going through this."

The adversities you face may differ from mine. However, you and I have this in common—our lives have had obstacles and the obstacles will continue to come. Your challenge might be:

- Overcoming an addiction
- Receiving a frightening medical prognosis
- Facing a financial failure
- Getting past a broken relationship
- Struggling to parent a difficult child
- Losing a child
- Confronting something in your life you have been repeatedly trying to change without success

- Dealing with something that still haunts you from your past

We can expect adversity as part of the very fabric of living. Though it may be unwelcome and unfair, it will come.

Many fall prey to the mistaken belief that being able to cope with and even thrive in the face of adversity—often called resilience—comes from natural, unlearnable traits that belong to only a select few. We can trick ourselves into adopting this self-limiting mindset because it is easier than doing what it takes to be resilient. Such actions are often hard and sometimes scary. Resilience, however, is under your control. It is a decision you can make.

DECISIONS THE RESILIENT MAKE

My first car was a twenty-five-year-old Chevrolet truck. The odometer (the instrument that counts the miles) had long since stopped working, so its mileage was a mystery. My dad had restored the engine, so it ran great. However, the exterior, even after a new coat of paint, showed the truck had lived a hard life.

It was the perfect car for a young male driver prone to making mistakes and make mistakes I did. I added scrapes, dents, and scratches to the already worn exterior.

The truck had a few idiosyncrasies. The starter—the part that cranks the engine when you turn the key—was faulty. I became adept at replacing the starter, and in the few years that I drove the truck, I went through several.

There were times when I turned the key, and instead of hearing the engine roar, I got no response. Ugh. That always made me anxious. As I sat in the truck, often away from home and unable to get the truck moving, I had two choices: figure out another way to start the car or sit and wait on a tow truck. As a teenage boy, sitting and waiting was torment because it meant missing out on life. It might have meant missing football practice, missing going to a friend's house, missing a date, or missing class. As long as I had a truck that would not start, I was missing out.

Another idiosyncrasy of this truck was I could start it without turning the key. It had a manual transmission, and my dad taught me how to "pop the clutch." With the truck in neutral, you could get it rolling and "pop" the clutch pedal —lift it until the gear caught the engine—and then quickly depress the clutch pedal, putting it back in neutral. If the car were going fast enough, the engine would spin, the car would start, and you could be on your way.

When I think about adversity, I remember that old truck. Like a truck that will not start, adversity can make us feel stuck and takes us off schedule. We miss out. If adversity causes us to sit out of life or become a lesser version of who we are meant to be, we miss out.

Some face adversity and cannot start the proverbial truck again. Two thousand years ago, there was a philosopher named Seneca. There will be more about him later. One thing he said was this:

While we are postponing, life speeds by. —Seneca (63 B.C.)[1]

Is that where you are? Is that where you are willing to stay? Is there an obstacle that has taken you off-track? Are you in an adversity that has you questioning whether you have what it takes to make it to the other side? Have you considered whether the hardship you are facing will make you a stronger person? Do you question whether that is even possible? Maybe it is not your own personal struggle that worries you, but you want to better teach resilience to someone you parent, coach, manage, or influence.

Resiliency is a decision. It is a decision you can make. Resilience is that *something* inherent in each of us—that little extra boost or reserve—that kicks in when we think we have hit the end of the rope. Believing in our resilience affects our behavior. The decisions we make affect the outcomes of our lives.

Resilience, however, is intangible and unmeasurable. It is hard to know how much resilience you have and what you can do to increase resilience if you lack it.

> RESILIENCE IS HOW YOU
> REACT, RESPOND, AND
> RECOVER.
> —JEFFREY GITOMER
> (2020)[2]

Resilience is not a fixed attribute. You can improve the skill with applied knowledge and effort. By emulating the habits and adopting the tools of resilient people, you can increase the velocity with which you bounce back. There are ways to *"pop"* the clutch, to kick-start resiliency, and to get past an adversity more quickly and effectively.

* * *

In the pages that follow, we will explore the decisions that resilient people make. I have observed these during two decades as a high-stakes trial lawyer working with people who were facing monumental obstacles in their life or business. I have seen decisions that lead to resiliency during a decade of coaching athletes in the competitive arena of high school and youth football in Texas. I also spotted them from the first-hand accounts of top performers, some in the public eye and some not, who encountered a volcanic eruption in life, navigated it, and came out stronger on the other side. They come from the recorded thoughts of slaves and emperors from centuries ago. I have also extracted lessons from interviews with people from all walks of life, including the following:

- A high school baseball coach with over 600 wins who got fired because of a political shootout.

- A financial wizard who drove a car over his own son.

- A mom and dad whose son did not survive birth.

- A single mom and cancer survivor given no chance for recovery.

- An elite-unit crime fighter that emerged from a home that stole his youth.

You may see pieces or perhaps even complete visions of yourself in these stories. Each of these survival narratives illustrates tools we can use to navigate the obstacles we face. These are tools of the resilient. These are the decisions they make.

This book tells the stories of people who faced different adversities and setbacks. Sometimes, the wounds were self-inflicted, and sometimes, they were not. Some setbacks were public. Some were not, but they were still embarrassing. Some people in the book are public figures and have shared their stories so others can learn from them. Others have much lower profiles, and their stories will be new to you. In all cases, the stories are compelling, encouraging, and instructive. They are here to give you heart to face the obstacles that appear in your path.

My father is in the construction business. When out on job sites with him, I noticed that some of the contractors work faster than others. They work with more energy. They are more productive and efficient. They get more done.

Often, these high-efficiency contractors wear belts with several different tools on them. When they are focused on a task, they have choices within easy reach. They can quickly match the right tool for the job at hand.

The decisions outlined in this book are tools the resilient use to overcome obstacles. Sometimes one will fit a problem better than another. However, like the best contractors, you will be equipped to cultivate resilience by mastering each of the tools and having them ready at hand.

* * *

The stories, encouragement, and teachings in this book revolve around a central premise. It is this: When you think you have exhausted all possibilities, remember this—you haven't.[3]

Years of working with and learning from business leaders, championship coaches, and high achievers in all fields have convinced me that we each have another gear, a second wind. When we tap into it, it can propel us past adversities, even those that seem insurmountable.

You may already have notable experience navigating and overcoming obstacles. You likely have something worth passing on to the proverbial travelers on the road behind you that are working through a hardship you have already conquered. Or, you may have an adversity even now that seems overwhelming. You may wrestle with questions like: *Can I get through this? Is this problem too big to solve? How can I survive this?*

Like most people, you probably have both situations. There are some obstacles you have conquered, but others you are still working through.

As we explore the decisions of resiliency, we will also identify three resiliency killers—the silent assassin called self-pity, the heavy fog of shame, and the masked bandit of resentment. These three emotions are common, but, left unresolved, they can rob our efforts to be resilient, to move on, and to overcome. However, we can resolve these three resiliency killers and put them into a proper context.

Wherever you may be in the path of your life, it is my hope and expectation that there is a message in these pages for you. Perhaps, there is a tool you had not used, or a fresh perspective you had not considered. Maybe you will discover an insight that brings you value and something helpful to navigate whatever hole you may be in. I hope you will decide to forge your resilience and become a toughness builder for someone you influence, manage, coach, or parent.

GETTING STUBBORN—SHAKE IT OFF AND STEP UP

A farmer had a donkey who had worked hard for many years in the fields but was getting old and suffered from poor eyesight. One afternoon, the donkey drifted into the back parts of the pasture and fell into a large, deep, abandoned well. The farmer had barricaded the well with rocks, but the donkey had broken through and did not see the hole. The well was so deep that the donkey could not get itself out. He brayed loudly. When the farmer heard the cries, he looked for the old donkey and eventually found it in the well. The farmer was frantic and tried to construct a plan to get the donkey out without harming or killing it. A neighbor came by to see if he could help. However, the well was deep and dark, and after hours of trying to find a solution, the two men finally decided that there was no way to save the donkey.

Stricken with grief, the farmer decided he should fill in the well so no one or no animal would ever fall in again. So, the two men shoveled dirt into the deep well.

As the donkey felt the dirt landing on him, it cried out in fear. Then, after a while, the crying stopped. The heartbroken farmer stared into the well to see the donkey one last time while his neighbor continued to shovel. What the farmer saw at first perplexed him. Then, it gave him tremendous joy as he realized what was happening. As the dirt fell down the well, it hit the donkey's back, and the donkey shook the dirt off and stepped up on top of it. The farmer grabbed his shovel and the two men continued to heave dirt down the well with as much speed as they could muster. They shoveled until the donkey got close enough to the top of the well to jump out and trot off happily into the pasture.

Life will throw dirt on us—all kinds of dirt, tough circumstances, unexpected and unwanted surprises, busted relationships, financial pitfalls, the deaths of those close to us, unfortunate health, and maybe even the consequences of our bad decisions. The secret to getting out of the holes of life is to shake off the dirt and then step up—shake off what is holding you back and step up to break through that obstacle.

Each adversity in life can be a stepping-stone. In the pages that follow, I hope you will find inspiration and the tools to shake off the dirt and step up. There is a way to the top of the well.

DECISION 1

DECIDE OBSTACLES ARE A VALUABLE PART OF LIFE

GRATED CHEESE AND VIDEO GAMES

As I was teaching my twelve-year-old son how to use a manual cheese grater, the thought came careening into my head—we live in a remarkable time. My son had never seen, much less used, a manual cheese grater. It was not because we do not use grated (or shredded) cheese in our family; we do. I like grated cheese a lot, in fact. However, we had never grated cheese by hand because we buy it in the store already shredded. On this day, though, we were using the manual cheese grater.

It was not the rotary grater with the crank handle either. That is almost like cheating. I was showing my son how to use the box grater, the cowbell-shaped device found in most kitchens for decades. My mom had taught me how to use it, and now I was passing this knowledge along to the next generation.

Each side of a box grater has a different blade arrangement, a long horizontal slicer, a knuckle-busting shredder, and the coarse and fine graters for hard cheeses and spices. For those unfamiliar with this menacing device, the user

1

scrapes the cheese or spice against the side of the grater while holding it firmly. Box graters do a fair job, but they can get clogged with the cheese. When this happens, the user's hand slips and scrapes against the grater. Accidental abrasions and cuts are common. Knuckles are particularly vulnerable.

As I reflected on the remarkable fact that my son had been missing out on a rite of passage—knuckle cuts from the box grater—I was reminded of how technology, specialization, and globalization have changed the way we live our day-to-day lives. Tiresome, thoughtless labor is replaced by a technical advance. We do not grate cheese today because we can buy pre-shredded cheese for close to the same price, thereby saving time and the wear and tear on the knuckles.

A lot of life is like our experience with grated cheese. Many time-consuming tasks that were necessary to survive are no longer part of our day-to-day lives. I dare say that few reading this book must cut a tree and start a fire to stay warm. You may do that for the aesthetic, but you also have the option to turn the thermostat on and have electric or gas-powered heat blowing through vents instantaneously.

Automating away slow and arduous tasks is remarkable, perhaps even miraculous. It frees up time to do things that produce greater value to society, our families, and ourselves. However, it also means that I do less hard things than my parents did, and my kids do less hard things than I did when I was their age.

* * *

One of the great things about video games is the reset button. Make a wrong decision? Just hit reset and start over. Went the wrong way? Hit reset and start over. Got surprised? Reset.

In a world with fewer cheese graters and more video games, we do less hard things, and we become more accustomed to hitting the reset button when things are not going well. Therefore, it should not be surprising that we are less resilient. After all, we have less practice at being resilient and grew up with games that taught us to hit reset when things did not go as expected.

Unfortunately, there are many things in life without a reset button. Instead, we must navigate the obstacles that befall us and live with the consequences of our choices. When life surprises us or we make the wrong decision, we do not get to start the game over or go back to the beginning and erase the decision.

Do you see the disconnect? In some areas of life, hard things are done for us and starting over is only one button away. In other areas of life, however, there is no reset button, and the work of overcoming adversity is hard. We should not be surprised at the struggle in building resilience.

Then, here is the real poison. When we live in a world with less and less adversity, we feel more and more entitled to living obstacle-free and worry-free. After all, when we peruse the profiles and timelines of the people we follow on social media, what do we see? We see highlights of a wonderful vacation; highlights of the day with a person's work, family, or friends; the equivalent of an ESPN "Top Plays of the Day" from our social network. It is easy to delude ourselves into believing that those around us are not feeling the same things we feel—uncertainty, disappointment, and lack of contentment. Life's challenges rarely make it onto Facebook or Instagram.

When we step back and really think about it, we know a social media profile is not reality. A vacation does not consist solely of highlights. It has those moments of frustration with delayed flights. It has kids repeating "how much longer" or "I'm bored" when we are already cranky after a poor night's sleep in a strange bed. Sometimes, the hotel's interior is not as nice as it looked in the pictures on TripAdvisor, and that same reality applies to family life, work life, and personal life.

We can fool ourselves into thinking life should be obstacle-free. However, obstacles are inherent in life. They are the very things that comprise the mosaic of our existence. These are things we tell stories about later. The obstacle forces us to grow and develop strength.

THE DANGER OF AN ON-DEMAND WORLD

The pace of life has changed in a remarkable way. What used to take twenty minutes to cook now takes one minute in the microwave. Amazon will bring almost anything to your door by the next day (if not the same day). We have access to any data in an instant via our smartphone. I can communicate with anyone, anywhere in the world via email or text message. A company half the world away can present a contract to me via their website to sign electronically and return within minutes.

It is no surprise that we have lost an important virtue—patience. Sometimes, it takes time and patience to get through adversity, to learn a new skill, to reform a destructive habit, or to build or restore a relationship. When we expect complex human issues and conflicts to resolve on the same expedited timelines where much of our life operates, we set ourselves up for failure. Resolving complexity takes time and patience. Resist frustration when it takes time to work through hard things and challenges.

* * *

A young boy was playing outdoors and found a caterpillar. As young boys like to do, he picked it up and took it home to show his mother. He asked if he could keep the caterpillar, and the mother said he could if he would care for it.

The boy got a large jar and put grass and leaves in the jar for the caterpillar to eat. He added a stick for the caterpillar to climb on. Every day, he watched the caterpillar and made sure it had food.

One day, the caterpillar climbed up the stick and started acting in a strange way. Worried, the boy called his mother, who recognized the caterpillar was building a cocoon, and she explained to her son something exciting was about to occur. The caterpillar was going to change into a butterfly.

The boy was beyond excited to hear about the changes his caterpillar was going to experience. He watched every day, anxiously waiting for the butterfly to emerge. Then, the boy noticed a small hole appeared in the cocoon, and the butterfly struggled to come out.

As the butterfly continued to struggle to escape the cocoon, the boy's excitement turned to concern. The butterfly was struggling so hard to get out and looked like it could not break free. It looked desperate, like it was making no progress.

The boy wanted to help, so he ran to find the scissors and then snipped the cocoon to make the hole bigger. The butterfly quickly emerged from the enlarged hole.

However, as the butterfly came out, the boy grew even more concerned to see the misshapen and swollen body and small, shriveled wings. He continued to watch the butterfly, expecting the wings would dry out, enlarge, and expand. However, the butterfly never changed. It spent the rest of its life crawling around with a swollen body and shriveled wings.

The butterfly could never fly. It had missed the struggle. A critical part of a butterfly's development is the struggle to push its way through the tiny opening of a cocoon. That struggle pushes the fluid out of its former caterpillar body and into its new butterfly wings. Without this process, the butterfly lacks the strength to take flight.

The same holds true for us. When we are young, we struggle to learn to crawl. It is then a struggle to learn to walk, talk, eat, and use the bathroom, but without that, we never develop the muscles or knowledge to progress. We accept that struggle for babies because we would never see a baby's struggle to walk as an issue. If we scooped the baby up and carried it across the room, we would not say, "Aww, poor baby, I don't want to see you struggle; let me just carry you."

Yet, some people think we should avoid struggle in adulthood. When we encounter an obstacle, we think, *Poor me. Why does this happen to me? I can't believe they put me in this situation.*

However, just as we learned and struggled with basic skills like walking and talking when we were young, advanced skills require extra effort and sometimes struggle when we are older. We push athletes to the edge and past their current training condition to expand their capacity. Young lawyers work on tasks above their skill sets to expand their knowledge and abilities. It is scary but also the surest way to learn and grow.

Our challenges and failures create growth. When training a muscle, it suffers micro-tears in the fibers, and the healing of those tears makes a muscle stronger and larger. Our lives are the same. The micro or macro tears leave us stronger, wiser, and more emotionally resilient once they heal. Surviving one storm gives us the confidence to survive another.

THE GREATEST GLORY IN LIVING LIFE LIES NOT IN NEVER FAILING, BUT IN RISING EVERY TIME WE FALL.
—NELSON MANDELA (1998)[4]

6

THE SILENT ASSASSIN OF SELF-PITY

Self-pity is a dangerous reaction to adversity. When adversity strikes, it is quite natural to feel sadness and disappointment. It is easy to feel sorry for yourself and your circumstances. Perhaps you even get angry. *If I am entitled to a life without obstacles, why do the obstacles keep arising? Where is the reset button?*

However, self-pity operates like a silent assassin. It kills our ability to get past adversity and rise above it. At some point, you must shake off the adversity, let the past go, make the choice that the adversity will not define you, and step out of self-pity. Otherwise, you preclude your ability to learn from the experience and to move forward in a constructive way. I am not addressing true clinical depression. Rather, I am talking about self-pity, "a self-indulgent dwelling on your own sorrows or misfortunes."[5]

When in the hole of self-pity, we become self-absorbed. It is destructive to dwell on negative events and continue to carry the bitterness and resentment. When we keep our focus on the hurt, we cannot focus on retaking control of our lives.

Worse yet, **if we blame negative circumstances for our place in life, we are giving up responsibility and control.** We whine and feel sorry for ourselves. Self-pity is a form of selfishness. It makes us less aware of the needs and suffering of others. Our suffering is all we think or care about in our self-absorbed state.

However, there is a choice. We can shake it off and step up. You are in charge of your happiness. So, feel the pain and the hurt. Live your reality, then let it go.

There is a Latin phrase: *Amor Fati.* It translates to: "Love Your Fate." It conveys a different meaning than the life wisdom gleaned from the poker table: "Play the hand you are dealt." *Amor Fati* is not a grudging acceptance of fate. Rather, it is a full-throttled embrace of present circumstances and a willingness to find the joy inherent in them. It means treating every moment—no matter how challenging—as something to embrace, not avoid. Just as oxygen is fuel to a fire, obstacles and adversity are the fuel to feed the fire of your potential. Marcus Aurelius was a Roman Emperor in the years 161 to 180 A.D. and a philosopher whose ideas have withstood the centuries. Aurelius' writings have experienced a renaissance of consideration over the last few decades. Aurelius, who is discussed more later in the book, wrote: "A blazing fire takes whatever you throw on it, and makes it light and flame."[6] This is *Amor Fati*—making light and flame out of every circumstance we encounter.

Adversity is not fun. Nobody wants to rebuild after a broken relationship, to return to a house with standing water in it, to dig themselves out of bankruptcy, or to get the frightening medical prognosis. However, when adversity strikes, we do not have a choice about what happened. Nor do we know where the adversity will lead. You may not have chosen the circumstance or want it. It may not even be your fault. And yet, here it is. Congratulations. Get to work.

Does that sound strange? Unrealistic? Too idealistic?

* * *

In the early 2000s, the game of poker boomed. Like many, ESPN's re-runs of the 2003 Main Event of the World Series of Poker captivated me. Chris Moneymaker (what a great poker name!), an amateur player from Tennessee, beat a field of 839 other players, including the best professional players in the world, to win the first-place prize of $2.5 million. I picked up the game and started learning and playing it.

I consider myself a serious amateur. I am certainly not a professional and do not have the skill set that comes from playing millions of hands. However, I have studied the game and have been fortunate to compete in some notable tournaments and games across the country.

Poker requires a high degree of skill to be successful over the long-term, but there is also enough of an element of chance that the superior player does not always win. There is always the possibility that the wrong card appearing at the wrong time can outdraw a superior hand.

In poker, you learn to think about hands in terms of probabilities. The best players either memorize or can quickly process the odds by which their hand is a favorite or an underdog to hands that other players may hold. When you start with pocket aces (the best hand) against pocket queens (the third-best hand), the player holding the aces will win 81 percent of the time or four times out of five. The aces are a vastly superior hand. However, statistically, the aces still lose one time out of five. Although most players know those percentages, when the aces lose, it still feels like a punch in the gut and that the world is out to get you.

Thus, at poker games across the country, there is a common occurrence: the "bad beat story." This is the tale of how the storyteller's superior hand got outdrawn by a low probability turn of events. You cannot be around a poker game for long before someone tells you how that last card, a mere 10 percent probability, ruined their night.

I have told some bad beat stories. The first time I traveled to Las Vegas to play in a World Series of Poker tournament, I went "all-in" with a pair of sevens (pocket sevens). I got called. The image of the player who called my bet is imbedded into my memory. In his mid-twenties and sporting a green mohawk, he called with an ace and a five. I had a 68 percent chance of winning the hand and doubling my stack of chips. However, when an ace hit the flop and no more sevens arrived, my tournament ended. It was a bad beat story of losing to a guy with a green mohawk.

However, I decided telling, and even more so dwelling on, bad beat stories was a waste of time. No one wants to hear my bad beat stories, and more importantly, dwelling on bad beats was harmful to my mindset while playing the game.

Focusing on the negative parts of variance affects both our mental state and our emotional state. Telling or not telling bad beat stories, whether in poker or in life, matters. Austrian writer Karl Kraus wrote: "Language is the mother, not the handmaiden of thought."[7] Our thoughts drive our words, and our words influence our thoughts. How we view luck and its role in our life has consequences in our emotional well-being and our decision-making. The lens through which we see variance influences the reality of events that happen to us and how we respond to them. *Are we the ones acting or being acted upon? Do we see ourselves as victims? Or do we see ourselves as eventual victors, even if bad things happen?*

Those who wallow in their bad beats and succumb to the silent assassin of self-pity miss the opportunity to overcome the bad beats. The self-pity kills the opportunities that arise to overcome the adversity. The preoccupation or mental focus on the unlucky card or the unfortunate circumstance prevents us from recognizing the arising opportunity.

Maria Konnikova, a psychologist, writer, and poker player, in her book *The Biggest Bluff*, calls it a "luck-dampener effect." She writes:

> *People get tired of hearing you complain. So, your social network of support and opportunities also dwindles. You don't even attempt certain activities because you think, "I'll lose anyway, so why try?" Your mental health suffers and the spiral continues. If you think of yourself instead as an almost victor, who thought correctly and did everything possible, but was foiled by crap variance, no matter, you will have other opportunities, and, if you keep thinking correctly, eventually, it will even out. These are the seeds of resilience, of being able to overcome the bad beats that you can't avoid, and mentally position yourself to be prepared for the next time.* [8]

As much as we might want events to go one way or another, our wishes have little bearing on the way things are. We may wish we had been taller, thinner, born into a rich or powerful family, that the special someone had fallen head over heels in love with us, or, at least, was the person we had idealized them into being. Despite our hard work, the less talented person got the promotion or won the game. The business deal fell through, or the grade came back lower than we expected.

What do we do? We think it is unfair, frustrating, and not right. However, it **is** life. So, how do we make the most of life when things happen to us that are out of our control? How do we make the most of bad beats when they occur?

We can get angry and announce our disapproval. We can throw up our hands, curse our fate, and tell whoever will listen about how unfair the events in our life are. None of that alters reality or adversity. So, how do we transform adversity?

In the days before the internet, when there were still traveling sales representatives, two shoe companies sent employees to a recently discovered remote island. When the two agents arrived, they discovered that none of the islanders wore shoes. The salesman for the first shoe company wrote back and said: "None of the residents here wear shoes. There is no opportunity. Will be returning immediately." The second company's saleswoman wrote back and said: "None of the residents here wear shoes. There is incredible opportunity. Please ship more shoes." The difference between opportunity and obstacle can be the way we view it.

> EVERY TERRIBLE THING THAT HAPPENS TO YOU HAS A HIDDEN GIFT AND IS LEADING YOU TO SOMETHING GREATER."
> —SARA BLAKELY (2014)[9]

Transforming adversity into joy and growth is strange and unrealistic for some. However, on the pages of this book, you will find many who did just that. They took adversity and turned it into success. The adversity became the fuel for their success. They embraced their circumstance, loved their fate, did not dwell on the bad beat, and then made brightness out of the darkness.

Just as dwelling on the obstacle can dampen our luck, the opposite is also true. Focusing on turning adversity into opportunity can enhance our luck. If you had a recent relationship that ended, but stayed in the game emotionally and relationally, your social network thinks of you when someone who is single and a good match pops up. If you find yourself in financial hardship and reach out for help instead of receding into a dark place, the good break is more likely to find you. While you cannot stop bad things from happening, you will feel happier and more content while you navigate life's vagaries. Your mindset of resilience will prepare you for the changes in variance that will come.

* * *

Glenn Mangurian rose through the ranks of an international consulting firm. He launched offices in Chicago and Germany and consulted with business leaders at General Mills, Dow Chemical, Hershey Foods, Citibank, and Procter & Gamble. Mangurian built a successful reputation and career and, as he entered his early fifties, was reaching his peak earning years.

Then, in May 2001, Mangurian suffered a sudden spinal cord injury that left him paralyzed from the waist down. He spent two months in a hospital and then another four years in physical therapy. Despite his injury, Mangurian remained active as a writer and speaker.

In 2007, Mangurian had an article published in the Harvard Business Review. He opened it this way:

> Those who have survived a traumatic, life-altering event often convey a curious sentiment: They wouldn't have it any other way. Some people emerge from adversity—whether a career crisis or a devastating breakup or a frightening diagnosis—not just changed but stronger and more content. They seem to have found new peace and even an optimism that they didn't have before. . . . Becoming paralyzed is without question the worst thing that has ever happened to me. I've had some very dark days, and life is a constant struggle. But at the same time, the experience has allowed me to take stock of all that I have, rediscover some of the neglected parts of my life, and cut through the clutter to focus on what really matters. Over the course of my hospital stay, I found the will to accept that my old life was gone and decided that I would create a new and equally meaningful one, drawing on all my experiences and a caring community of family and friends. Today, I've not just returned to consulting; I've also engaged in endeavors that wouldn't have occurred to me before, such as advocating for stem cell research.[10]

Mangurian's story is a full-throttled embrace of present circumstances and a willingness to find the joy inherent in them. It is *Amor Fati,* taking the bad beat and then bouncing back with a winning hand.

Accept that life is not perfect. In fact, welcome the obstacle. Do not fear the scraped knuckles from grating the cheese or expect you will transform from a caterpillar to a butterfly without struggle. Do not even wish for it. Your struggles make you who you are and allow you to blossom into something more. Give up the search for the reset button. Forget the bad beat. There is a butterfly waiting on the other side of your struggle.

DECISION 2
DEFINE YOUR LIFE

THE RESILIENCY DECISION

R esilient people decide they are going to be in control of their lives and not allow circumstances to take control. This first decision is critical.

OBSTACLES CAN DEFINE YOUR LIFE, OR YOU CAN DEFINE YOUR LIFE BY HOW YOU RESPOND TO THEM.

Adversity is like the hinge on a door. Left unchecked, adversity can shut doors. However, we can resist the closing door. We can push against adversity in the same way we can push against a closing door and open it into the opportunities on the other side.

There is a powerful thought pattern in Jack Canfield's book, *Success Principles*, that illustrates the importance of our choices when adversity strikes.[11] It is expressed as a formula:

$$E + R = O$$

The **E**vents that happen + our **R**esponse to those events = the **O**utcomes of life. When an adverse **E**vent occurs, we get to choose how we **R**espond. We can let our adversities define

14

us, or we can choose our **R**esponse to our adversities and create a different narrative. Throughout the book, the first letters in the words **E**vent, **R**esponse, and **O**utcome are capitalized and in bold type to illustrate how resilient people can change the **O**utcome of an adverse **E**vent by their **R**esponse.

For many people, an adverse **E**vent dictates the **O**utcome. The non-resilient **R**esponse is E = O. The adverse **E**vent, the adversity, controls the **O**utcome without interference.

However, because we get to choose, we can influence and dictate the ultimate **O**utcome by how we respond to the adverse **E**vents in our lives.

* * *

The venerable CBS show, *60 Minutes,* featured an interview with an opera singer named Ryan Speedo Green.[12] Speedo grew up in a rough part of Virginia with an abusive mother in low-income housing, next door to a crack house. Speedo developed into a frustrated child unable to manage intense anger that often manifested into destructive behavior. By fourth grade, Speedo's school decided to move him to the class for delinquent children. Once there, he threw his chair at the teacher, Elizabeth Hughes. For most teachers, that threat would be enough to end the teacher's interest in the student, and understandably so. However, Mrs. Hughes's interest only grew, and she began to plant the seeds of life change in Speedo.

Mrs. Hughes took an interest and took the time to learn about Speedo's circumstances. While school became a safe haven, trouble at home continued. During the same fourth-grade year, he threatened his mother and brother with a knife. The police responded and removed Speedo from his home. They took Speedo down three flights of stairs in shackles and handcuffs, stuffed him into the back of a police car, and took him to a juvenile detention facility located hours away. He spent two months in the facility.

While he was there, Mrs. Hughes called. Twenty years later, Speedo still remembers what she said: "Don't let this moment define you. This doesn't define you. You can be better. You can do better."[13]

While locked away, Speedo took steps toward a positive Response that would ultimately determine his Outcome. A facility caseworker and a psychiatrist took an interest in Speedo, and he listened. When released, he moved with his family and got a fresh start in a new town with new friends. Soon, he got involved in new activities, including chorus. Once Speedo discovered he had a unique gift for singing, and after much work, he was accepted into Virginia's prestigious Governor's School for the Arts. At fifteen, he took a life-altering field trip to the Metropolitan Opera in New York City and saw *Carmen* with Denyce Graves, a woman of color in the title role.

Speedo recalls: "At that point in my life, I thought opera was like, you know, for white people. And the lead character, the title role, was a person who looked like me—a person of color. It completely shattered all my preconceptions of what I thought opera was."[14]

Speedo fell in love with opera. He returned home and announced to his voice teacher he would one day sing at the Metropolitan Opera. The voice coach gave Speedo a list of items he had to do to fulfill that dream: graduate high school, go to college for music, sing in foreign languages. Green methodically worked through the entire list, including a bachelor's and master's degree in music. At twenty-four, Speedo entered a Metropolitan Opera competition for young singers. He beat more than a thousand other contestants.

Today, Speedo Green is an award-winning performer. *The New York Times* described him as a "scene-stealing bass-baritone with a robust voice."[15] He regularly performs at the Metropolitan Opera, just as he predicted at fifteen.[16]

Green's life is a powerful illustration that the Events of life—even the adverse ones—do not have to define us or dictate our Outcomes. Mrs. Hughes's words of advice are powerful: "Don't let this moment define you." Speedo lived out an inspired Response that became an inspiring Outcome.

This book outlines the tools for living an inspired Response. However, making an inspired Response starts with the decision that an adverse Event or circumstance will not have the last word. Instead, the difference is in the decision to make an intentional Response.

Recall the skilled and efficient contractor with every useful tool of the trade: a top-of-the-line power saw, a highly advanced digital level, a laser guided measuring tape, the finest nails, and a hammer perfectly fitted for the worker's hand. The contractor's tools are of no use, however, until the decision is made to use them.

Like the woodworker who stares at the unfinished product, there are many who numbly stare at a problem. They feel shame at their Event and prefer to hide it rather than overcome it. Seeking to overcome will require disclosure and the risk of embarrassment. Shame has a powerful way of clouding our judgment and convincing us to keep our problem hidden and unresolved. The fog of shame is discussed more in the section about Decision 4.

At other times, we feel resentment toward someone whom we perceive caused or created the problem. Or the silent assassin—self-pity—creeps in and we utter phrases like, *"Why does this always happen to me? Why am I so unlucky?"* As long as we have someone to blame and can feel sorry for ourselves, we will never get past the obstacle. The masked bandit of resentment is discussed in the section about Decision 12.

Shame, resentment, and self-pity are like poison to resiliency because they prevent you from taking ownership of your obstacle. You can choose to let the adverse Event define you. You can choose, instead, to define yourself by your Response to the Event.

The tools of resilient people like Ryan Speedo Green are throughout the book. Will you decide to use them?

DECISION 3

DECIDE TO RUN UNTIL THE SECOND WIND ARRIVES

OUR BODY'S INCREDIBLE ABILITY TO KEEP GOING

"I'm going to run a marathon. Do you want to join me?" The question came from Jennifer, my wife, and there was only one correct answer. It was the year we both turned thirty, and we had just been through five tough years. We had been trying without success to have a child and had gone far down the rabbit hole of infertility treatments, continual cycles of doctor visits, testing, shots, bad news, and disappointment. It was physically and emotionally draining for Jennifer, and I lacked the emotional intelligence to understand what she was feeling, much less to be truly empathetic. We were both young professionals trying to find our footing in our careers. I had done a poor job of setting boundaries at work and had been unavailable when she needed me.

The marathon question came when we stopped the infertility treatments. I was not yet a truly empathetic spouse, but I knew how to answer her.

Although I have many blessings in life, having a runner's physique is not one of them. Running long distances is difficult, and it is not something I do for fun. However, I was trying to be a supportive husband, so we signed up for a training program and a marathon.

It was cold the day of our race. That morning, we woke up to sub-freezing temperatures and sleet. We had trained during the warm spring and summer months, but the event was in December. I was not adapted to the cold.

The race started fine. Jennifer and I ran the first twelve miles together, and we were pacing as we had trained. Then, at mile twelve, adversity struck. I got a cramp in my midback that restricted my breathing. Whenever I tried to inhale deeply, I cramped and could only take shallow breaths. I had to stop and walk to slow my breathing and stop the cramping.

However, after a few minutes of walking, my body temperature would drop, and I would get the chills. So, I had to jog again to warm up. Then, the cramping would return, and I had to slow down and walk. The cycle continued: slow down, speed up, slow down, speed up, cool down, cramp up. After a few miles and seeing this was throwing Jennifer off rhythm, I suggested that she go on ahead of me and finish her race. She did, and I continued with this same slow down and speed up rhythm.

For several miles, I struggled. I thought about quitting. If the van that picks up injured runners had happened by at just the right time, I might have hopped on.

Slow down, speed up, slow down, speed up. This continued until mile twenty.

In marathons, mile twenty is often called the "wall." It is where many runners encounter trouble. Their bodies start to break down. However, mile twenty was just the opposite for me that day. When I got to this point in the race, it was like a switch flipped. The cramping stopped, and I could breathe normally, even while jogging. Something in my body adapted, the adversity lessened, and I finished the race.

Endurance athletes refer to the point where the body adapts as "catching a second wind." Wikipedia defines it this way: "Second wind is a phenomenon in distance running, such as marathons or road running (as well as other sports), whereby an athlete who is out of breath and too tired to continue suddenly finds the strength to press on at top performance with less exertion."[17] That day, I experienced a second wind that propelled me through the adversity and to the finish line.

From my observations and experience, the second wind is not limited to our physical bodies. We can catch a second wind in our emotional, psychological, and spiritual selves as well. I have witnessed the second wind arise in response to many types of adversities. I have seen it come to those who have overcome incredible obstacles, failures, embarrassments, and losses.

When adversity first arises, it can appear insurmountable. However, as we push against an obstacle and decide adverse circumstances will not defeat us, the obstacle becomes more manageable. Solutions to the problems appear.

Just as our body adapts to physical exertion even when winded or exhausted, our mind adapts as we push against and into our struggles. The Germans have a word for it: *Sitzfleisch.* Translated literally, *sitzfleisch* means "sitting meat" or "sitting flesh." It is a term for one's behind. However, the term means a great deal more than the physical part of the body. Having *sitzfleisch* means having the stamina—the staying power—to work through a difficult situation. A cruder translation is having the ability to stick your butt to the seat and not leave until you have completed the job. This indomitable will or force of purpose is inside each of us. It is a response of power.

THE DEMON WHO KEPT SHOWING UP

Dumas is a remote town at the top of the Texas panhandle. The largest employer is a meatpacking plant, and the dominant landscape features are large wind turbines catching the stiff Texas breeze and converting it to electric power. Dumas is part of the high Texas plains once ruled by Native American tribes, such as the Comanches, known as tough and brutal fighters. The settlers of Dumas had to be hardy and brave to survive. That DNA still runs through the town.

Some of the biggest community events each year are the home football games on Friday nights when the Dumas High Demons take the field. The population of Dumas is about 14,000. There are about 1,100 students enrolled at Dumas High. The football stadium seats 7,000. The town shuts down on Friday nights in the fall to watch its young people on the team, cheer squad, drill team, and in the band.

Football practice each year starts around August 1, and the townspeople circle the date on their calendars. As preparations for the season begin, the talk in the offices, barbershop, restaurant, courthouse, and town square focuses on how the Demons might fare this year. The late summer weather is hot with highs reaching the mid-nineties most days.

A few days before practice started for the 2018 season, the Demons offensive line coach, Antonio Murga, went to see a doctor for pain just below his sternum. He thought it was related to his diabetes medication. The doctor took an ultrasound, then a CAT scan. Murga was not expecting what he heard next. The doctor told him that the scan revealed several tumors that were sure signs of pancreatic cancer. He would need a biopsy.

The diagnosis was dire: Stage IV cancer. It was spreading to his other organs. In addition to a mass on his pancreas, there were spots on his liver. The doctor would say there were "too many to count."[18] Chemotherapy treatments were to start immediately.

For those in even the most sedentary professions, trying to work during energy-draining chemotherapy treatments can be difficult. For an offensive line coach trying to keep up in the August practice heat, it seems impossible.

Yet, Murga showed up day after day. On the second day of practice, he spoke to the team, "I'm not going to miss anything, and I expect the same from you."[19] Every two weeks, Murga took the forty-five-mile trip for a five-hour chemotherapy session. Murga said his doctors hit him with the strongest treatment available. He then drove back to Dumas, took a nap, and went to practice.[20]

Murga said, "I'm just always tired . . . That 2018 season, I hardly walked anywhere. I would have the golf cart to go everywhere. I sat on the sidelines, would pull a cooler up and sit."[21] *Sitzfleisch.* Staying power. Indomitable will.

Going into the 2020 season, Murga continued to receive treatments, and he continued to coach. He said, "I'm going into my twenty-second year of coaching, and I always told my boys that adversity is going to pull a knife on us but we're going to pull a machete. I had two options, I could stay here and just die or I could practice what I preach; no matter what happens, we've got a job to do. Life happens. I went to work."[22] *Sitzfleisch.*

Dumas's Head Coach, Aaron Dunham, explained Murga this way: "He exemplifies everything that we're trying to instill in our football program. He would get chemo treatment in the morning and then come to practice and just love and coach his kids with everything that was inside him. At times you'd look over on the side of the field and he's throwing up. He's been an inspiration for our kids, our staff and this entire community."[23] The adverse Event—the cancer—did not define Murga.

Coach Murga passed away during the 2020 season. He coached for 22 years in schools across the Texas and Oklahoma panhandles. In his obituary, his family wrote this:

"Through his fight with cancer, he showed people how to persevere and how to fight the good fight. He continued to show an extraordinary amount of commitment to his team and players by coaching even through his treatments."[24]

The Dumas High Demons had good seasons in 2018, 2019, and 2020. They won most of their regular-season games and a few playoff games. However, the accurate measure of a coach's success is not solely the team's won-loss record. The greatest measure of success is gauging what the coaches have instilled in the players and how that radiates out over the span of the players' lives. For the players in Dumas, no matter what life throws at them, they had the example of Coach Murga, who showed up day after day with his stubborn refusal to let circumstances derail his mission. They know toughness can overcome even the most difficult of adversities.

Sitzfleisch. Find your second wind. Continue your **R**esponse.

DECISION 4
DECIDE TO CONNECT WITH OTHERS

THE WISDOM OF PEOPLE WITH SCARS

Scars. I have a few. There is one on my right hand from a surgery to repair a broken bone, and there's one on my right shin from a bad fall. The one on my right knee is from a mishap on the ski slope that resulted in a torn ligament.

> THERE IS TREMENDOUS POWER WHEN A PERSON WITH A HEALED SCAR HELPS ANOTHER WITH A FRESH WOUND.

I bet you have a few scars, too. My wife has a scar on her left knee that tells the story of the pain and discomfort of a surgery to repair her anterior cruciate ligament in the days before arthroscopic surgery. It reminds her of the long rehabilitation to regain the strength in her leg and to reteach herself how to move, run, and jump. That scar was also the conversation starter I used when I met her. (Miraculously, she married me anyway!) Her scar tells a story.

My dad has a scar on his neck from a scary encounter with the sharp top of a cyclone fence that barely missed crucial arteries and air passages. Enough time has passed that the story can be told with humor.

Not all scars are visible. Sometimes, we bear the invisible scars of a broken heart, broken dreams, and a broken spirit. There might have been a time in your past when you experienced a significant loss, survived a catastrophe, or you escaped from a harmful, dysfunctional relationship. Combat veterans may return with no visible wounds, but they still struggle with the pain of post-traumatic stress. Emotional scars are real.

However, a scar begins as a wound that requires expert care. A mistake in wound care can cause the spread of infection to other parts of your body. An open wound can even spread disease to other people if they get too close. The transition from the wound stage to the scar stage is an important part of healing. For emotional wounds, it is vital to find someone who has already navigated the journey. A powerful tool of the resilient is a connection to other people from whom they can draw wisdom and support.

As my wife and I neared the end of our struggle to grow a family, we met another couple at church, Terry and Janet Grimm, who had been through the same struggle. Meeting the Grimms was divine intervention for us. They were willing to be vulnerable and share their struggle with infertility and their ultimate choice to adopt a son. Though we knew little about adoption, the Grimms provided two things we acutely needed: hope and a practical roadmap for dealing with the obstacle we were facing.

HOPE

In the midst of adversity, it can feel like you are alone. Connecting with someone who has already successfully navigated your obstacle offers the comfort of knowing you are not alone and can succeed.

One of my phobias is being caught in a storm while on a ship at sea. It is a bit of an irrational phobia as I live several hundred miles inland and rarely ride on a boat. However, I imagine being a captain and trying to navigate through a storm. If I were able to talk to someone via the on-ship radio, I think I could maintain composure and hope. However, if the radio were to go out or no one could communicate with us, I feel certain the dread would set in.

These are the same thoughts when trying to navigate a figurative storm in our lives. We feel hope when we connect to someone who has navigated the storm ahead of us. However, without a connection, we can feel alone and unsure we can make it through. By contrast, when we have a connection with someone who has successfully overcome the obstacle, it offers comfort and hope.

Roger Bannister was an English runner who was the first to break the four-minute mile barrier. He achieved the feat in a race on May 6, 1954, with a time of three minutes, fifty-nine and four-tenths of a second (3:59.4). Some of the most brilliant coaches and gifted runners in North America, Europe, and Australia had been trying to run a sub-four-minute mile since at least 1886. The shadowy mark remained elusive. Most experts had decided the four-minute mile was beyond human capability.

However, once Bannister broke the mark, the once impossible achievement became routine. Just forty-six days after Bannister's feat, John Landy, an Australian runner, completed a mile in three minutes, fifty-eight seconds. Then, just a year later, three runners broke the four-minute barrier *in a single race*. Over the last half-century, more than a thousand runners have run sub-four-minute miles. Today, it is not even newsworthy when an athlete runs a mile in less than four minutes.

What made the impossible suddenly attainable? It was not a sudden acceleration in the physical evolution of runners or new training techniques. Rather, the mindset changed. Until Bannister did the *impossible*, runners did not have the mindset to surpass the four-minute mile. When Bannister broke that limit, the others now believed that they *could* do something they previously had been told they *could not* do.

For us, the Grimms were tangible proof that there was a path to navigate through our obstacle. The Roger Bannisters and Terry and Janet Grimms of the world give us hope.

PRACTICAL ROADMAP

Connection with others during adversity provides a practical roadmap to navigate our obstacles. Consulting with or getting support from another with experience often yields valuable insight or a solution we had not considered. They may tell us what roadblocks to expect as we navigate the road. There is great value in just knowing what emotions we might encounter, so we are braced for them as they arise on our journey.

Terry and Janet Grimm showed us how adoption could work. This led to meeting other people, including adoption experts who taught us how to adopt and parent the child well. Their stories gave us hope and led us to a way forward.

Consider the map application on your smartphone. When you are preparing the path to an unknown location, the map shows the most efficient way and keeps you from taking wrong turns. The map can even tell you of unexpected issues, like construction or wrecks blocking your path.

Cartography or mapmaking has been an important part of human history from the beginning. In ancient Babylon, Greece, and Asia, cave painting was used for exploration of new terrains. Throughout the centuries, we have used maps as an essential tool to help us define, explain, and navigate our way through the world.

The same is true for your struggle. There is someone who has already walked your journey. They have a map to help chart a path and avoid wrong turns and obstacles along the way.

THE FOG OF SHAME

Shame is one of the major barriers to resiliency and connection with others. Brené Brown, one of the foremost researchers, speakers, and authors on the effects of shame, defines it this way: " . . . the intensely painful feeling or experience of believing that we are flawed and therefore unworthy of love and belonging—something we've experienced, done, or failed to do makes us unworthy of connection."[25] Our feelings of shame are amplified when we perceive our adverse circumstance is something we created, such as an addiction, financial failure, or a broken relationship.

In the Garden of Eden, the last description of Adam and Eve before they were tricked by the serpent was "they felt no shame."[26] What a remarkable feeling! This was part of the idyllic nature of the Garden to feel flawless, lovable, and worthy. There was no fog and nothing to distract from the true vision of God's intention for us to feel no shame.

Then, once tricked by the serpent, they immediately felt shame about their nakedness, so they put on clothes to hide. When they next heard God, they tried to hide among the trees.[27] The response of Adam and Eve to their initial feelings of shame still plays out today. Shame causes us to want to hide. It distorts our thinking. When we most need connection, shame drives us away from it.

We do not want to reach out because we fear embarrassment or what people will think of us. However, this is often a misplaced fear. Authors Jerry Wyckoff and Barbara Unell call it the Twenty-Forty-Sixty Rule:[28]

At age twenty, you worry about what others think about you; at forty, you don't care what others think about you; and at sixty, you realize no one was ever thinking about you in the first place.[28]

Releasing shame is a critical step to resilience. When engulfed in shame, our clarity diminishes, and our ability to move beyond adversity is compromised.

The Texas Hill Country is a beautiful place. It is hilly, full of trees, and brimming with all kinds of wildlife—deer, wild boars, wildcats, coyotes, and birds. Recently, I had a dinner meeting in one of the wonderful Texas Hill Country towns, Fredericksburg. I had to leave Fredericksburg early the following morning before the sun rose. Overnight, a thick and low fog had descended on the Hill Country. As I drove on the narrow roads, my headlights did little to illuminate the path ahead. The fog was so thick it made driving difficult and treacherous. I had trouble seeing more than a few feet ahead of the windshield and had to drive slowly. It would have been easy to drift off the road because of the fog blocking my vision.

When shame sets in like a thick fog, decision-making is difficult and treacherous. Shame clouds our judgment, blocks our vision, keeps us from seeing the reality in front of us, and separates us from those who might illuminate our path. Our shame keeps us from connecting with someone who could help us.

On the foggy morning drive, I was grateful when the sun rose and warmed the air enough to burn off the fog. The same is true for us when walking through adversity. Someone who has overcome adversity can help us stay on the path and avoid obstacles along the way. However, connecting with others when we are in the midst of adversity requires us to be vulnerable and admit we need help because we have made a mistake. That's hard to do, especially when we feel shame about our situation.

Isolation—whether real or perceived—is a terrifying feeling. That is the source of my stranded-at-sea phobia. It is also a destructive feeling, but it is not the same as being alone. Isolation can descend like the Hill Country fog, even when we are with other people. When shame drives us to isolation, it locks us out of human connection and makes us feel powerless to change. Shame-induced isolation is the fog that clouds our vision from the path ahead.

A first step is connecting to others—even amidst our shame—and recognizing the universality of our most private struggles.[29] You are not alone. Someone else has walked a similar path. Centuries ago, the Israeli King Solomon wrote: "What has been will be again, what has been done will be done again; there is nothing new under the sun."[30] Becoming vulnerable to seek help and guidance is jet fuel to resilience.

As he entered his mid-30s, Taylor Conroy had been wildly successful. He started his career as a firefighter and pivoted to real estate investing, where he built a million-dollar business. After a life-altering trip to Kenya, he founded Change Heroes, a unique online charitable funding platform. In its first year, Change Heroes raised over $1.4 million that helped fund 140 socially beneficial projects around the world. Taylor was asked to speak and share his idea with influential people and large crowds in venues across North America, including the United Nations, Harvard, and New York University. He was lauded in elite circles for his social entrepreneurship.

However, Change Heroes began to struggle. Taylor poured everything he had into keeping it viable, including his life savings, and he accrued a mountain of debt. His efforts failed, and he filed for bankruptcy. Taylor went from feeling adored to feeling embarrassed.

While still in the midst of the bankruptcy, Taylor opened up and become vulnerable. He called a videographer and shot a two-minute video where he announced Change Heroes had failed and filed for bankruptcy. When describing it a few months later, he said while his "stomach [was] churning, I posted it to Facebook and sent it to my entire contact list." Taylor says the responses were "unexpected and incredible." Some people called, saying they were experiencing "rock-bottom" challenges, and Taylor's vulnerability reminded them they were not alone. Others called to encourage him and shared how their challenges had been instrumental in shaping their character and "making them better human beings."[31]

This kind of vulnerability—broadcasting an embarrassing failure to your entire contact list—is almost unimaginably hard. For Taylor, he said it was freeing. When we can break from the shame of what others might think about our struggles or failures, we can connect to find the resources that will help us be resilient.

A Word for Men

As men, it can feel like we are trapped in a box. We often experience conflicting expectations. Though we are criticized for not expressing our feelings and allowing ourselves to be vulnerable, when we do display the courage to be vulnerable, we are shamed for not being "manly." For many, the Response to this dilemma is to shut down, lash out at others, or drown frustrations in alcohol or other addictions. When we feel shame, it is easy for us to become highly self-absorbed.

Here is a word of encouragement: The "man code" that leads too many of us to feel inadequate and engulfed in shame is not a display of toughness, and it is not the way to be truly resilient. It is only a barrier to stepping into the fullness of our potential and what we were created to be.

We can live with integrity and not fear our failures or how others might perceive us. Through the connection gained by our vulnerability, we will find others that have been down the same path and have suffered the same wounds. When we become unashamed to express our humanity rather than just our toughness, we can grow into the best version of ourselves.

* * *

On April 23, 1910, Theodore "Teddy" Roosevelt gave one of the most widely quoted speeches of his career. Roosevelt had left the White House in 1909 and spent a year hunting in Central Africa before embarking on a tour of Northern Africa and Europe in 1910. He attended events and gave speeches in Cairo, Berlin, Naples, and Oxford. He then stopped in Paris on April 23 and delivered a speech to thousands of people. Roosevelt titled the speech "Citizenship in a Republic," but the talk was later referred to as "The Man in the Arena."[32]

In addition to speaking about his family history, war, human rights, property rights, and the responsibilities of citizenship, the former president railed against cynics who looked down at those who were trying to make the world a better place. "The poorest way to face life is to face it with a sneer," he said. "A cynical habit of thought and speech, a readiness to criticize work which the critic himself never tries to perform, an intellectual aloofness which will not accept contact with life's realities—all these are marks, not . . . of superiority but of weakness."[33] Then, he delivered an inspirational and impassioned message that drew huge applause:

It is not the critic who counts; not the man who points out how the strong man stumbles, or where the doer of deeds could have done them better. The credit belongs to the man who is actually in the arena, whose face is marred by dust and sweat and blood; who strives valiantly; who errs, who comes short again and again, because there is no effort without error and shortcoming; but who does actually strive to do the deeds; who knows great enthusiasms, the great devotions; who spends himself in a worthy cause; who at the best knows in the end the triumph of high achievement, and who at the worst, if he fails, at least fails while daring greatly, so that his place shall never be with those cold and timid souls who neither know victory nor defeat.[34]

Resilient people use failure as a tool to greater success. Every scar has a story. What tales of resilience will your scars declare?

DECISION 5

DECIDE TO FIND YOUR PURPOSE

THE ANCHOR IN THE STORM

D arin leaned across the table over our respective cups of coffee and said, "I've shared mine. Now, what are *your* core values?" Wow. I had no answer. Even though I worked at a law firm with core values and even had core values for the football team I was coaching, for myself, I had no answer. Reality struck. I had never considered what my personal core values were, much less what they should be.

Core values have become a buzzword in businesses across the globe. At times, the entire notion of core values can be a running joke, because business leadership often does a poor job of connecting the employees to their core values and explaining their importance to the organization and its mission. Therefore, core values become nothing more than words on a fancy poster in the break room.

However, the notion of *personal* core values—knowing who you are and what things are important to you—carries tremendous power. The root of the word "core" is the Latin word *cor,* which means heart. Our core values are those values stamped upon our hearts. They are not intended to be fancy words on a poster, but values of who we are or strive to be.

Identifying your core values carries many benefits. Here are two: It will force you to be intentional about answering a critical question—what things in life are most important? Then, your answer to that question can help with making later decisions. Ask yourself if the activity you are contemplating aligns with your core values. If so, then it is a good decision. If it does not align, leave it alone.

Darin survived a heart attack at a relatively young age and emerged with a new appreciation for living life with intention. I understood living life with intention in theory, but my theoretical understanding had not spurred action. Darin understood it in practicality, and it compelled him to ask himself hard questions, uncover what was important to him, and live life in response to and in alignment with his purposes and values.

So, when Darin asked me, "What are your core values?" and I had no answer, I was convicted to go through the process of identifying and writing them down. I spent parts of several days in introspection asking, *Who am I? What do I want to be? What do I want my life to be about? What is important to me?* It was a valuable process, and at the end of it, the answers became clear:

- I am a disciple.

- I am a great husband.

- I am a great father.

- I make a positive difference in the world around me.[1]

The section about Decision 8 discusses the importance of the words "I am" and the words that follow them. The phrasing of my core values ("I am", "I make") is sometimes more aspirational than a reflection

As I reflected, my values became evident quickly. For the first few years after writing them down, they did not change. However, I am open to my values morphing over time or, more likely, to a new value appearing. Indeed, in recent years, I have added one: *I will be better today than I was yesterday.*

Determining my core values, writing them down, and reminding myself of them helps me stay centered in who I want to be. This becomes a driving force that aids in overcoming adversity.

That driving force—living out our core values—is also what builds courage. Courage requires a core, and the Latin concept of heart (*cor*) is at its root. Courage is the emotion that bubbles up from our core, from our heart. Courage is found in the conviction that comes from our core values.

The concept that courageous people have no fear is often misunderstood. People who act with incredible courage are not immune to fear or discomfort. They feel those emotions and sensations. However, something drives them past the fear or discomfort. There is a core value, something bubbling up from their heart, that allows them to overcome the fear or discomfort.

The stories of resilient people are always marked by courage.

* * *

Jenny Mulks had been experiencing pain in her abdomen for ten months. She was recently divorced, raising a young

---

of reality. Often, I fall short of what I aspire to be. However, one of the most powerful words in any language is the word that follows "I am," because that defines how you see yourself, and your self-concept will govern the Outcomes in your life. Since I put my core values on the wall of my office to remind myself of them often, I phrased them so they were not merely aspirational ("I want to be") but defining ("I am").

son alone, and working full time in medical sales. The two doctors she consulted both told her the abdominal pain was related to life stress. One day, the pain was unbearable, and she ended up in the ER. Eight hours passed in the cold ER where Jenny was surrounded only by curtains while the doctors tried to find the source of the pain. Finally, at one o'clock in the morning, a doctor came through the curtain. Without raising her eyes from the chart she held in her hands, she said, "You've got metastatic liver cancer. You have a massive tumor in your liver, and we don't know the point of origin."[35]

Jenny's mother, who had been sitting with Jenny, mustered in a shaky voice, "What are her chances?" The doctor looked up and held up her forefinger and her thumb less than an inch apart with the unspoken, devastating message: slim. Symbolic of the little light creeping through the small space between the doctor's fingers, Jenny felt the light of life escaping her body, mind, and soul.

Her mind swirled, and her heart sank. Gabriel, her young son, dominated her thoughts. As Jenny said, her biggest fear was not dying; it was "leaving behind my four-year-old innocent child, my son."[36]

After the diagnosis, Jenny spent the next two weeks bedridden. She saw five different doctors. Each had a similar prognosis—six to twelve months to live.

However, Jenny had a dominating force. In her *cor*, she had an overpowering desire that Gabriel grow up with a mother. She says: "I awoke to what was happening."[37] She was feeling powerless, allowing her life to slip without a fight. But her desire to be there for Gabriel caused her to pivot. She sought out a treatment team who had a plan. Though she lived in California, she selected a doctor at the renowned M.D. Anderson Cancer Center in Houston, Texas, and began the year-long journey of treatments to eradicate the cancer.

It was a tough year. She had difficulty sleeping and got into a routine of going outside to her porch at four o'clock in the morning. She called it her "time with God" and her "self-preservation time."[38] She read, watched the sun come up, and reveled in the simple joy of watching different colors each morning at dawn as light spread across the Nine Sisters, the mountain peaks in and around her hometown of San Luis Obispo, California.

Jenny was intentional about staying around positive conversations, even to the point of asking friends and family to stop talking about her illness or the status of her treatment in front of her. She set boundaries to protect her heart, spirit, and soul from negativity. Years later, she would reflect that she was generally not good at establishing boundaries, however, during this period, she was. She became proactive and driven to protect her son.

She also dug into her relationship with God. As she slowed down and became focused on staying positive, seeing the joy in simple things, and fighting the cancer, she discovered an unusual peace and manifest presence of God. Even while she was being wheeled into surgery and before she knew if the cancer could safely be removed, she felt the presence of God. She recalls feeling angels with her in a way she had never seen or felt before. The feeling was so powerful that she began to cry when sharing the story with me over ten years later.

Jenny found spiritual resources she had not known were there. She found the courage to do what was necessary to place her mind, heart, and spirit in positive and healing states of being and found the resilience to overcome. The story has a happy ending. With the help of the Lord, her family, and her team of medical professionals, Jenny defeated the cancer. She also let it change her.

Jenny has a new perspective and appreciates life more. Life's daily obstacles bother her less. In 2013, Jenny left her corporate position to start a non-profit organization, Along Comes Hope. Jenny and her team provide support to families of children with cancer. They provide financial assistance for treatment, emotional support programs, and advocacy for policy change to better support these families. The website for Along Comes Hope can be found at www.alongcomeshope.com. Jenny's *cor*, her heart for Gabriel, gave her the courage to be resilient in the face of a hopeless prognosis. Her core value compelled her to fight the cancer. It inspired her **R**esponse that led to a positive **O**utcome.

* * *

Jeremy and Tami were high school sweethearts. However, they came from different worlds. Jeremy was the son of a Baptist pastor, which might seem like the setting for a stable childhood, but sometimes pastors are not great husbands, and they are not great dads. Tami was the daughter of an alcoholic and carried that baggage. To survive, she had to be tough. They got married out of college, but issues quickly emerged.

As a financial wizard, Jeremy made a career of managing large, employee retirement-plan portfolios. He is gifted at making money multiply and commands a top salary for his services. He grew up in a house without much money. His dad's position did not pay well, and his mother stayed home to raise the kids. So, as Jeremy's salary grew, he wanted to make up for lost time and use money for enjoyment.

Though Tami also did not grow up with much money, she was content to live frugally. Money in the bank meant security, something she had little of growing up. Jeremy and Tami's conflicting views on how to use their money caused tension. They both describe themselves as stubborn.

There were disagreements about more than money. They had a son shortly after getting married. Tami wrestled with being a mom and requested more help around the house. Jeremy worked a demanding job and did not hear the requests of a young mother trying to hold it all together. The story he created and then told himself was that his wife would never be satisfied with him or his contributions to the household. Besides, his vision of fatherhood was influenced by his father and did not involve substantial participation in running a household.

Although Tami was pregnant with their second son, the strain between them continued and, eventually, Jeremy moved out and left Tami alone with their young son. Living on his own in an apartment, Jeremy was restless and had trouble sleeping. He was searching and wrestling with questions like: *What is really important? What do I want out of life?* He lay awake at night, furiously typing a journal as he searched for answers. He had his computer read back his thoughts until he could nod off to sleep. He was hunting for his *cor*.

Their second son was born. Jeremy got the news from his mother, who told him Tami was on her way to the hospital. He made the trip there, but Tami did not want him in the room with her because of her anger and disappointment with Jeremy. The chasm between them was too wide.

They did agree on the baby's name, Adam. He was born prematurely and had to spend some time in NICU before being released from the hospital. While anxiously waiting for Adam to be released, the coldness between Jeremy and Tami began to thaw. Tami eventually agreed Jeremy could hold their new son. Then, she agreed Jeremy could move back home.

They described the first year back as "really rough."[39] Once their trust had broken, it was not easy to rebuild. Tami was still very guarded, and Jeremy expected to hear he was not good enough again. However, they started putting the bricks back into the proverbial wall that had been torn

41

down. Then, one fateful day, the unthinkable happened and became the glue with which they rebuilt their relationship.

At eighteen months old, Adam was playing in the garage. Jeremy had to run an errand and jumped in his car, not knowing Adam had crawled behind his back tire. When Jeremy backed up and heard Adam scream, he immediately stopped the car and sprinted to the back. His wheel was on Adam's head, and the boy's face was turning purple. Jeremy frantically pulled Adam free, summoning supernatural strength.

However, Adam was not breathing. By this time, Tami had heard the commotion and yelled for help. A neighbor heard her screams and called 9-1-1. They brought Adam to the front yard and started trying to revive him. The paramedics arrived and got Adam breathing again. He had a broken collarbone from being pulled from under the car but was otherwise unhurt.

Imagine the horror of running over your young son. Jeremy had to carry that with him. From the accident, a pivotal moment in this family arose. This type of Event could tear their fragile alliance apart. Instead, it drove them together.

The Event sent Jeremy—who was already coming to the realization that being a husband and a dad was his true *cor*—diving into that purpose and figuring out how to make it work. He called the Event the "grand finale reminder" of the blessings he was close to losing. As they went to doctors for test after test to ensure that Adam was recovering as he should, each visit further clarified Jeremy's vision for what he wanted for himself and for his family.

Tami said the Event made everything click for her. She felt a surge of compassion for Jeremy and witnessed how much he loved their boys and how almost losing Adam affected him. She became incredibly supportive of Jeremy in his vulnerability, and he returned the support.

The near catastrophe became the bridge. As Adam healed from his physical injuries, Jeremy and Tami began to heal from their emotional wounds. Their **R**esponse to the **E**vent became a clarity of focus that elevated the importance of their family relationship above the imperfections they had previously focused on in each other. The **O**utcome is a beautiful family that remains together with two thriving boys. Jeremy and Tami now minister to and counsel other couples struggling in their marriages.

* * *

One of the great upsets in modern sports history occurred on February 11, 1990, in the Tokyo Dome in Tokyo, Japan. This was the night when and the venue where Buster Douglas knocked out Mike Tyson.

James "Buster" Douglas began boxing professionally in the 1980s and was considered a talented fighter, but he lacked the motivation to become a champion. In the year before his fight with Tyson, he committed one of the cardinal sins of boxing. He reportedly quit during a match.[40]

By contrast, Tyson had become the youngest heavyweight champion in boxing history when he was only twenty years old. Nicknamed "Iron Mike," Tyson intimidated other boxers with his fast, powerful punches. Going into the match with Douglas, Tyson seemed invincible. He had a 37-0 win-loss record and had won thirty-seven of his matches by knockout. In the fight immediately before his match with Douglas, Tyson had knocked his opponent out a mere ninety-three seconds into the bout.[41]

The match with Douglas was to be a tune-up for Tyson before he was to fight the leading contender at the time, Evander Holyfield. Tyson's victory was such a sure thing that most Las Vegas sportsbooks would not even offer odds on the fight. The few that did priced Tyson as the 42-1 favorite, meaning that someone betting on Tyson would have to wager forty-two dollars to win just one. Tyson was, in the eyes of all the experts, a virtual lock to win. During the broadcast of the event on HBO, the announcers relayed a story that encapsulated the prevailing view of the fight. Upon his arrival in Japan, one of the Associated Press reporters assigned to cover the event had been asked by customs officials how long he was going to be working in the country. He responded: "Oh, about ninety seconds." Like this reporter, everyone expected Tyson to knock out his opponent quickly. Douglas was introduced on the HBO broadcast as "the next victim of the Mike Tyson fighting machine."[42]

One of the few people who believed in Douglas was his mother, Lula Pearl. She was initially opposed to her son fighting Tyson and tried to convince him not to take the match. But when she watched her son explain how he could beat Tyson, she saw something in him that made her change her mind. In the months leading up to the fight, Lula Pearl told her friends that her son could indeed defeat Tyson.[43]

Then, tragedy struck. On January 18, 1990, only three weeks before the fight with Tyson, Lula Pearl suffered a stroke and died. Some people tried to talk Douglas into postponing the fight, but he was adamant that he wanted to go forward.

When the fight began, Douglas opened aggressively. This was a different scene than Tyson's preceding fights when it appeared the opposing fighter was intimidated and fighting scared. Douglas played to his strength with a quick and accurate jab that prevented Tyson from sparring in tight with him. When Tyson was in close quarters, he was the most dangerous. When Tyson tried to get inside, Douglas tied him up, moved away, or immediately hit Tyson with multiple punches as he came within Douglas's reach. Douglas later said fighting Tyson that night was a relief. Dealing with the death of his mother had "built [his] strength." He "was getting ready to be a nightmare to [Tyson]."[44]

It quickly became apparent that this was not going to be another easy and quick Tyson victory. As the fight progressed, Tyson managed to land a few of his signature and threatening uppercuts, but Douglas still dominated the fight. Tyson's left eye began to swell from Douglas's jabs. In the eighth round, Douglas dominated until the last few seconds when the announcer on the HBO broadcast, Larry Merchant, noted: "Douglas is asking of Tyson, some questions he hasn't been asked before...in the last few rounds of a fight you have to come back and win it."[45]

Within the last ten seconds of the eighth round, Tyson, who had been backed onto the ropes, landed a big uppercut that sent Douglas to the canvas. For so many of Tyson's opponents, this would have been the end. Most did not get back up after Tyson had knocked them down. However, on this night, Douglas was driven by a compelling force—the memory of a mother who believed in him. He staggered to his feet just before the referee got to the terminal count of ten. As Douglas regained his footing, the eighth-round bell sounded to end the round, and Douglas was able to return to his corner to recover before resuming the fight.

In the dramatic ninth round, Tyson came out aggressively, hoping to end the fight and save his title. Tyson and everyone watching assumed Douglas—previously labeled a quitter—would still be hurt and vulnerable from the eighth-round knockdown. However, Douglas was determined and successfully fended off Tyson's attack. What followed next is what some boxing experts have called one of the greatest rounds in heavyweight fighting history. Both men traded punches before Douglas connected on a four-punch combination that staggered Tyson. He fell back to the ropes, hurt and penned in. Douglas closed in and unleashed a vicious flurry of punches to try to knock Tyson out. Despite Tyson's attempts to back Douglas off, he could not. Douglas's attack continued until the round ended.

In the tenth round, Tyson opened with a strong right hand but was visibly weakened from the accumulation of punishment absorbed throughout the match. Tyson's left eye was swollen shut. One minute into the round, Douglas hit Tyson with a few jabs before landing a devastating uppercut that snapped Tyson's head upward. As Tyson reeled back from the uppercut, Douglas immediately followed with four punches to the head. Following that barrage, for the first time in his career, Tyson fell to the canvas. In a famous scene caught in a widely distributed photo, Tyson fumbled for his mouthpiece before finally sticking one end in his mouth with the other end hanging out. He attempted to get back up, but the referee reached the decisive count of ten before Tyson could find his feet.[46] Douglas had become one of the most unlikely heavyweight champions in history.

Surrounded by the frenzy in the ring during the interview immediately after the fight, Douglas was asked how he won the fight no one thought he could win. He broke down in tears. Through his sobs, he said: "Because of my mother ... God bless her heart."[47]

Douglas had an incredible driving force that night—the memory of his mother, Lula Pearl. She was his *cor*, the one who believed in Douglas, even when everyone else had written him off. This central motivating force drove Douglas off the mat when so many who had fought Tyson in the past could not regain their footing. This *cor* gave Douglas courage and allowed him to do what everyone thought was impossible.

* * *

Have you identified your core values, your central motivating force or forces? We do not lose heart because of adversity; we lose heart because we forget why we are doing what we are doing.

Viktor Frankl, a survivor of the horrific concentration camps during World War II, wrote a landmark work in 1946 titled *Man's Search for Meaning*. In his book, he shared his observations on life deeply engraved by his experience at the Auschwitz death camp.

Frankl observed and later recorded his views on why some captives survived, while others died. He pondered why some with good health, intelligence, and survival skills did not survive, but others who lacked these attributes endured and lived. Frankl concluded that the single most significant factor for survival was a sense of a future vision. The survivors had a mission, a *cor* that gave them inexplicable courage and resilience.

I hope no reader of this work faces adversity to the same level Frankl did. However, I do hope the lessons he learned and shared can be deeply embedded. Resilient people have a strong connection to what motivates and is important to them. When a motivating force from their *cor* drives a person, obstacles become mere bumps in the journey.

If you have yet to put your core values down on paper, I encourage you to do so. Spend some time praying and meditating over the questions: *What is really important to me? What do I want my life to look like?* Other insightful and sobering questions to reflect on are: *What do I want people to say at my funeral? How do I want to be remembered?*

If you have a trusted friend or family member, this is a powerful exercise to do with someone. Ask them: *Based on what you see and know about me, what are the things that are the most important to me?*

As you are going through this exercise, ask people who you respect or admire the "million-dollar question": *What do you know now that you wish you knew twenty years ago?* Brian Cain, one of the leading sports performance consultants, tells the story of asking the "million-dollar question" to Mack Brown, a phenomenally successful football coach for the University of Texas and the University of North Carolina. Coach Brown responded by saying, "Sailing the right ships."[48] Coach Brown explained that he used to value championships but had learned to value relationships. The million-dollar question will often unearth valuable wisdom.

Once you have ascertained your core values, write them down and post them where you can see them. Internalize them. Decide there is no obstacle too large to prevent you from living your core values. As the obstacles grow, the attachment to a motivating core value must also become bigger.

DECISION 6
DECIDE TO TRANSFORM YOUR PAIN

ADVERSITY ALCHEMY

While studying the resilient, a commonality kept appearing I had not expected. Many people who demonstrated powerful resiliency had transformed their adversity into a central motivating purpose. The adversity defined the *cor* discussed in Decision 5. Just as the ancient alchemist tried to purify and transform base metals (such as lead) into precious metals (like gold), the resilient had a unique ability to transform the pain in their lives into a driving force for societal good.

Angela Duckworth is a Professor of Psychology at the University of Pennsylvania and the author of an incredible book, *Grit: The Power of Passion and Perseverance*. Therein, she shares one of the major findings of her grit research: people with a sense of purpose were "grittier"—they were more likely to push through adversity and obstacles.

Many of the compelling stories of resiliency involve people who took their focus off themselves and the obstacle that engulfed them. Instead, they actively sought to serve others as a way to cope with the pain of their experience. There is a general truism that most people experience joy when helping others. This seems inherent in the human experience and speaks to the way we are created.

Being myopic in our adversity to the exclusion of seeing and feeling empathy for the people and the greater world around us only serves to increase our difficulty on the path to healing and wholeness. When we zoom out, see the problems of others, and choose to address them, the adversities we face appear and become more manageable.

In April 2018, Desiree Linden became the first American female in thirty-three years to win the Boston Marathon. That achievement was remarkable enough, but how she did it was even more remarkable. The 2018 race was marked by horrible weather. In the early hours before the race, it was cold and snowing. As race time approached, the weather warmed to just above freezing. The snow turned to bone-chilling rain. To add to the runners' misery, a strong cold wind blew. The runners were soaked and fought the cold wind that chilled them to the core.

Linden was an accomplished runner. She ran her first Boston Marathon in 2007, and she placed nineteenth. She finished second in the 2010 Chicago Marathon and second in the 2011 Boston Marathon by a mere two seconds.[49] She also finished second in the 2012 U.S. Olympic Marathon Trials. Although she started the 2012 marathon in London, Linden had to withdraw during the race due to a stress fracture in her femur. She finished tenth in the 2014 Boston Marathon and fourth in the 2015 Boston Marathon. In 2016, she again placed second in the US Olympic Marathon Trials and then seventh in the Olympic Marathon in Brazil. She finished fourth in the 2017 Boston Marathon.[50]

Linden had a career that any distance runner would envy, but she never had the experience of crossing the finish line first in a major race. As she started the 2018 Boston Marathon, she ran alongside her friend and one of the top runners in the world, Shalane Flanagan. Just six months prior to the Boston Marathon, Flanagan had won the 2017 New York City Marathon.

In the early stages of the race, Linden struggled. In an interview after the race, she said she was not feeling well and had considered dropping out mid-race. Instead, she chose to stay in the race and try to help Flanagan by running with her, blocking the wind, and helping Flanagan stay on a winning pace. In fact, in the beginning of the race, Linden slowed down and held back while Flanagan made a bathroom stop so Linden could help Flanagan catch back up to the pack.[51]

As Linden helped Flanagan get back to the lead pack, Linden's race began to turn. Runners dropped out because of the extreme conditions, but Linden got stronger. Linden found her second wind. She made her way to the lead pack. Then, she took the lead. Linden went on to win and, post-race, she sent out a Twitter message that said: "Sixth time is a charm. Keep showing up."[52]

There are many powerful messages from Linden's performance, like the power of continuing to show up time after time. However, another observable tool from Linden's performance is the buoying power of helping someone else. Had Linden become focused on the subpar way she felt, she likely would not have even finished the race. Part of Linden's success was her decision to help Flanagan. It was part of what kept her going until her second wind kicked in. Linden said: "When you work together, you never know what's going to happen. Helping [Flanagan] helped me."[53]

The motivation to care for another is a strong driving force, like the single mother who keeps going day after day after day, driven by the love of her children. Jenny Mulks' story in the preceding section is a prime example of how a mother's love gives her a resiliency superpower. Likewise, the spouse caring for her aging partner who is no longer able to care for himself has a driving force. Similarly, there is the soldier who faces unspeakable horrors but continues because of his love for the others in the unit.

Resilient people have the willingness and ability to take their eyes off themselves and whatever obstacle they are facing. They find empathy and care for others. There is undoubtedly a part of the human experience where caring for others brings fulfillment and energy.

Desiree Linden's experience in the 2018 Boston Marathon proves the grit research of Professor Duckworth. Linden's experience over a few grueling hours in Boston is a microcosm of what can happen to adversity that we face in any other area of life. As we zoom out and away from our problem to a higher purpose, we become grittier and more resilient to adverse circumstances.

* * *

Germaine Gaspard is a servant warrior. He is a tough man who does tough things and has a gentle smile. His parents divorced before Germaine was in the first grade. Germaine's dad became a single father who suffered with drug and alcohol addictions and left Germaine isolated and alone.

Germaine says he ran away from home because he wanted to be found. He often contemplated hurting himself to bring the pain in his heart to the surface. He spent a lot of time at the Boys & Girls Club. When the club closed and no one was there to pick him up, he remembers the hushed tones of adults whispering. "It happened again." He was taken to a child protective services facility for a time.

His father once disappeared for a seven-day stretch. Germaine, suffering from the pains of hunger, found an uncooked turkey in the freezer. After putting it in the oven for thirty minutes, he ate the still raw turkey for dinner. At the age of thirteen, Germaine witnessed a school shooting. He was friends with the shooter, the girl that was shot, and the intended victim.

In the midst of this pain, Germaine says he began to find his power. He was determined to learn how to defend himself. Growing up among rival gangs and racial tension, he made the decision to find life and live it on his terms.

Germaine went into law enforcement. He served in the elite special operations group of the Texas Rangers, a storied law enforcement team in the State of Texas, fighting narco-terrorist gangs and human traffickers. The once-frightened boy built a career protecting others. He also served as the vice-president of a nonprofit organization that fed 75,000 children over a six-month span. The once hungry child now feeds other hungry children.

Germaine has coached youth teams in football and track from tough and under-resourced neighborhoods and is the founder and CEO of the Good Life Living Group, whose mission is to build effective leaders and teams. The boy too-often forgotten by his father now stands in the breach to be a father figure to hundreds of children that are like he once was.

Germaine had a choice about how to respond to Events that were far from ideal. He felt real pain from those Events, but he did not let that pain overtake him. He used it to drive him.

In his March 2019 TEDx Talk, Germaine shared with the audience that everyone has an origin story:

The story that you whisper to yourself. It is the story that only you hear. It is a story of victim or victorious . . . Greatness comes from willpower. The will to do the hard thing. The will to make yourself responsible and to respond with your abilities, rather than your complaints or your settles . . . I stand here not in spite of my experiences, rather, because of my experiences. My experiences birthed resiliency and **resiliency is my superpower.**[54]

Germaine's resiliency is driven by providing others with all the things he lacked as a child.

* * *

I met Mark Jacobs in college. He was bright, personable, and engaging. It seemed clear that he had a bright future ahead of him. Mark married his college sweetheart, Chelsea. She was equally impressive and had a heart for children. After graduation, they married and moved to Dallas. They were living the life they had dreamed about. Mark was doing well for a pharmaceutical company, and Chelsea was the star teacher at a pre-school. Mark and Chelsea already had three beautiful girls when they found out they were going to have a boy. They decided to name him Chase and prepared his nursery. His sisters were excited about his pending arrival.

However, a few weeks before Chase was due, Mark and Chelsea got the prognosis that no parent wants to hear. Chase had died inside the womb. In the days immediately after the heartbreaking news and having to deliver her stillborn son, Chelsea could not bring herself to leave home. She was terrified of awkward encounters with family and friends who were not sure how to react. She remembers one pregnant friend at the time running in the other direction to avoid an encounter. "You just realize this is never going to be the same. No one is ever going to see me the same."[55]

Well-meaning friends and family doled out grief books. Chelsea made it through a few. Instead of continuing through the growing stack, they read books and stories about children in Africa. Mark and Chelsea were struck by the poverty in which countless children live. Their hearts hurt for the thousands of orphans left behind because of HIV, genocide, or neglect.

Mark remembered a light-bulb moment. "Why have I not been brokenhearted over this like I was brokenhearted over the loss of my son?" The couple encouraged family and friends to honor Chase by sponsoring a needy child. "Really quickly when we started reading, our heartbreak turned," Chelsea says. "Our grief was still there, but it just changed shape."[56] What a powerful phrase—the grief changed shape. What a powerful emotion—the grief changed shape. What a life-altering **R**esponse to an **E**vent—the grief changed shape.

Mark and Chelsea became the living embodiment of what Angela Duckworth saw in her grit research. They became people propelled by a sense of purpose, something larger than themselves, advocates for radically transforming the lives of children in dire circumstances. Like those in Professor Duckworth's research, this act of digging into a higher purpose and one larger than themselves made Mark and Chelsea grittier and gave them the fortitude to push through the tragedy in their lives. Instead of an **E**vent that could have destroyed their lives and marriage and created a scar that would never heal, it became the catalyst for change in the lives of people Mark and Chelsea had not yet even met.

Before long, this little movement to honor Chase grew. Six years later, the non-profit Mark and Chelsea started, His Chase, provides education for 250 children in Rwanda. Through their work and the support of others who have joined them, His Chase provides school and stability for children left in challenging situations after the genocide of the mid-1990s. Children aided by their programs have finished school, attended college, gotten married, and started families.

We see stories like Mark and Chelsea's and are drawn to them. They resonate on a heart level. How do some people encounter a tragedy, an obstacle, or an adversity and turn it into a breakthrough, an area of growth, something beautiful? How do we take whatever adversity we are walking through and transform it? How do we take ugly **E**vents and transform them into beautiful **O**utcomes?

Mark and Chelsea Jacobs could have been that couple who lost their baby. Instead, they became that couple who started a powerful ministry. They became emotional alchemists and transformed their pain into a blessing for kids who needed a blessing. It is very brave.

Do you have the courage to use your pain, to devote yourself to a purpose larger than yourself? A purpose larger than your adversity? A purpose that will change the shape of the grief, the resentment, the sadness, the lostness you may be experiencing? Shake it off, step up, and see if your adversity will drive you to your second wind.

DECISION 7
DECIDE TO TAKE THE LONG VIEW

THE WISDOM OF A BREAK-UP, A FARMER, THE STOICS, AND A PRISONER

A springboard to resiliency is perspective. One of my sons had his first girlfriend in eighth grade. They texted, talked on the phone, and gathered groups of friends to go to the movies. However, as happens with most young loves, the relationship ended. My son was devastated. Although my wife and I knew breaking up was the inevitable outcome of the relationship and another love would come and wash away the pain of this breakup, he could not see it that way. We knew this was but the first step in the long journey to finding *the one*, but our son did not yet have that vision.

He lacked the perspective to understand this breakup would not be the end of his journey to find a companion. It was only the first step, and he will probably remember it, but the difference between how he viewed the breakup and how we viewed the break-up was based on experience and the perspective such experience brings.

When adversity arises, we often get so focused on the adversity that it blurs our vision of its true place in our overall life. Many adversities are short-lived, and though they control the moment, they impact only a small sliver of our overall life. Even long-term adversities do not take away many of our blessings and gifts. It is like owning an orchard of beautiful trees with one that is diseased. The diseased tree certainly deserves our attention, but it does not change the many other beautiful trees in the orchard. Resilient people can see the whole orchard without becoming hyper-focused on the problematic tree. When we undergo trauma and the disruption of our routine—especially when it's sudden—we become preoccupied with trying to make sense of what happened. An important element of a resilient perspective is understanding that hardship and adversity often lead to greater things.

THE FARMER

One day in late summer, an elderly farmer worked in his field with a horse that was old and sick. The farmer felt compassion for the horse. So, he let it loose to go to the mountains and live free for the rest of its days.

Soon after, neighbors from the nearby village visited and offered their condolences. "What a shame. Now your only horse is gone. How unfortunate you are! You must be incredibly sad. How will you live, work the land, and prosper?"

"Who knows? We shall see," the farmer said.

Two days later, the old horse came back rejuvenated after meandering in the mountains while eating the wild grasses. Not only that, but he also came back with twelve new, younger, and healthy horses that followed the old horse into the corral.

Word got out in the village of the old farmer's good fortune, and it was not long before people stopped by to congratulate the farmer on his good luck.

"How fortunate you are!" they exclaimed. "You must be very happy!"

Again, the farmer softly said, "Who knows? We shall see."

At daybreak the next morning, the farmer's only son set off to train the new wild horses, but he was thrown to the ground and broke his leg. One by one, villagers arrived during the day to bemoan the farmer's latest misfortune.

"Oh, what a tragedy! Your son won't be able to help you farm with a broken leg. You'll have to do all the work yourself. How will you survive? You must be sad," they said.

Calmly going about his usual business, the farmer answered, "Who knows? We shall see."

Several days later, a war broke out. The emperor's men arrived in the village, demanding that young men come with them to be conscripted into the emperor's army. As it happened, the farmer's son was deemed unfit because of his broken leg.

"What very good fortune you have," the villagers exclaimed as their young sons marched away. "You must be very happy."

"Who knows? We shall see," the old farmer replied as he headed off to work his field alone.

As time went on, the broken leg healed, but the son had a slight limp. Again, the neighbors came to pay their condolences.

"Oh, what bad luck. Too bad for you."

The old farmer simply replied, "Who knows? We shall see."

As the war dragged on, the young village boys died, and none returned. The old farmer and his son were the only able-bodied men capable of working the village lands. The old farmer became wealthy and was very generous to the villagers. They said, "Oh, how fortunate you are. You must be very happy."

The old farmer replied, "Who knows? We shall see."[57]

This classic story of the farmer illustrates a mindset that allows us to be free from or unattached to conditional happiness or unhappiness based on the circumstance of the moment. Conditional happiness lacks the perspective of the bigger picture. It is an obstructed vision. We see only a small snapshot in a longer movie, and we judge the movie based on one frame out of a million.

Every Event is part of a larger whole. The meaning and nature of any Event—what is judged to be good or bad—is only relative to the changing circumstances and conditions surrounding it. We often fail to consider the whole picture or apply the perspective of a longer time period, a larger forest, or the whole movie.

> HAVE YOU EVER WONDERED WHY THE SOLUTIONS TO OUR FRIENDS' PROBLEMS ARE SOMETIMES SO OBVIOUS TO US, YET THEY CANNOT SEE THEM?

The reason we sometimes struggle to find solutions is our lack of perspective. Our initial reaction when we run into an obstacle is often an emotional reaction. When an adversity arises, the emotions of frustration and anger cloud our judgment and ability to be objective. Our frustration and anger hinder our internal ability to solve a problem or find a solution. However, when we look at someone else's problems, we do not suffer from the same emotional barriers and can perceive their problems objectively. Our clear head, unburdened by negative emotions, allows us to see more clearly, react accordingly, and see solutions.

When many people hear friends or family discuss an upcoming home remodel project, they assume the project will be over budget and take longer than expected. However, those same people convince themselves *their* project will be under budget and will finish early. This phenomenon, known as Solomon's Paradox, is a common malady. We can reason more wisely about other people's circumstances than our own.

King Solomon, the third leader of the Jewish Kingdom, is remembered as a man of boundless wisdom. People traveled great distances to seek his counsel. He wrote one of the great Biblical books of wisdom, Proverbs. Despite his knowledge, his life was messy. He made bad decisions repeatedly, had uncontrolled passion for money and women, and handed the kingdom to his ill-prepared son, who ruined and divided the nation. Hence, Solomon's Paradox. Plenty of wisdom for others, but not for oneself.

Train the skill of being your emotionally detached friend, your problem solver. Imagine hearing your story for the first time, trying to counsel yourself on how to get past that obstacle, keeping in mind your skills and assets, but setting negative emotions to the side. Easier said than done. This is part of the reason connection to others (discussed in the section about Decision 4) is so important.

When adversity strikes, a lens of inequity clouds our vision and judgment. *Why did this happen? Why me? What could I have done to prevent this?* Or worse yet, *who can I blame for this?* Similarly, questions about an uncertain future will flood our thinking: *What does this mean? How can I go on? What will happen to me?*

Ultimately, it is fruitless to wish to change the past. It is debilitating to try to figure out uncertainty in the future. The question of "why me" is a waste of energy. You can control only the present and the actions you take now to get past or through the adversity you are facing. The perspective of "What can I do right now?" leads to resilience. Going back to the section about Decision 2, the thing we can control is our **Response**. Focusing on the **Response** leads to resilience.

THE STOICS

I am not a philosopher. However, I have been intrigued by what I know of the philosophy of Stoicism, a school of thought in Athens, Greece in the early 3rd century B.C. One of the basic tenets of Stoicism is that the path to happiness lies in accepting each moment as it presents itself. Many Stoics believed living with virtue and thinking with reason led to inner tranquility—a state of mind "marked by the absence of negative emotions such as grief, anger, anxiety, and the presence of positive emotions—in particular, joy."[58] Stoics believed tranquility, not happiness, was the ideal state of mind achieved by cultivating a calm indifference to your circumstances. A chief way to do this was to lean into negative emotions and experiences, not shun them. Rather, such emotion should be closely examined and understood.[59] This ability to be tranquil, even during negative experiences, is the foundation for the phrase "stoic calm."

To better understand the Stoic philosophy in practice, consider the life conditions of three of the leading voices of the philosophy—Epictetus, Seneca, and Marcus Aurelius. Each came from vastly different positions of power and influence in their communities. Epictetus was a slave, Seneca was a political advisor, and Aurelius was an emperor. However, the three men had a commonality—extraordinarily difficult circumstances that forced them to dig deep for ways to overcome and find resilience.

Epictetus was born into slavery. His name literally means "acquired." Later in life, he obtained his freedom and taught philosophy in Rome. However, he was banished from Rome by the emperor Domitian and fled to Greece. Throughout his life, Epictetus suffered from a disability in his leg likely caused by a break or injury from his master during his time as a slave.

Seneca was born into an influential family and quickly ascended the social and political ranks until exiled by the

Emperor Claudius on charges of adultery with the emperor's niece. In a bizarre twist, Claudius's wife secured permission for Seneca to return and become the tutor and adviser to her son, Nero, who became one of the most notorious and tyrannical emperors in the history of the Roman Empire. Seneca's death came when Nero suspected Seneca of plotting against him and ordered Seneca to commit suicide.

As a teenager, Marcus Aurelius was handpicked to be placed into the line of succession to become leader of the Roman Empire. He is widely regarded as one of the "Five Good Emperors."[60] During Aurelius's reign, Rome faced wars with multiple nations and tribes, both civilized and barbaric. Rome was also terrorized by a fifteen-year plague (believed to be either measles or smallpox) that caused up to 2,000 deaths a day. The historian, Cassius Dio, a third-century Greek senator who wrote a history of Rome, described Aurelius this way: "[Marcus] was not strong in body and was involved in a multitude of troubles throughout practically his entire reign. But for my part, I admire him all the more for this very reason, that amid unusual and extraordinary difficulties he both survived himself and preserved the empire."[61]

Perhaps it is unsurprising that a philosophy arising from the life experience of these three men has, at its foundation, the idea that it is not what happens to us that makes us sad, anxious, or angry. Rather, it is what we believe about what has happened to us that governs how we feel. The Stoic philosophy is that external Events are not negative in and of themselves. Rather, it is the belief we hold about external Events that causes suffering, or, alternatively, joy.

Most of us think it is the Events of life that make us sad, anxious, angry, or depressed. We allow our mind to be controlled by the thoughts: *It would be so much better if this had not happened. Why did this have to happen to me?* Yes, it might have been easier if the bad thing had not happened, if the employee had listened, if your parents or in-laws respected your boundaries, if your neighbor wasn't so obnoxious, or if your kids did their homework without a battle every night.

However, the Stoics argue that these external Events are not negative in and of themselves. What causes our emotions and suffering are the beliefs we attach to the external Events. While a stubborn employee, overbearing parents, obnoxious neighbors, or rebellious children are not preferable, sometimes they are the reality. You can bemoan, blame, or try to escape it emotionally.

Or . . . you can see this as a chance to have a hard and necessary conversation. It could be knocking on your neighbor's door and talking to him or her without losing your temper, counseling your employee, teaching your child a tough lesson, or having a discussion with your parents that ultimately enhances the relationship.

Aurelius said, ". . . things have no hold on the soul. They stand there unmoving, outside it. Disturbance comes only from within—from our own perceptions."[62] The Stoics did not dread hard things; they embraced them. It was a chance to step up and practice courage. Allowing an Event to disturb us can occur only if we permit it. Though it might not be desirable to lose money, to lose a friend, to fail, or to be criticized, how do those things affect us? It does not deprive us of our chance to Respond. Our character remains intact.

Ultimately, how we feel about Events, whether they be good or bad, is within our control. We choose the emotion we assign to the Event. Though we do not get to stop bad Events from occurring, we do get to control how we Respond to

> IT'S FORTUNATE THAT THIS HAS HAPPENED, AND I'VE REMAINED UNHARMED BY IT-NOT SHATTERED BY THE PRESENT OR FRIGHTENED OF THE FUTURE. IT COULD HAVE HAPPENED TO ANYONE. BUT NOT EVERYONE COULD HAVE REMAINED UNHARMED BY IT. —MARCUS AURELIUS[63]

those Events. This includes how we feel about the Event and how we let it affect us.

When a bad Event happens, we often begin to imagine the worst. A bad review at work causes us to imagine losing our job, having our car repossessed, having our house foreclosed upon, and being unable to buy food. We imagine a cascading chain of horrible Events. Though the odds of the cascading chain of horrible Events happening are small, we become preoccupied with them, and they create anxiety and stress within us. Worse yet, they create self-pity—one of the obstacles to resilience. In the section about Decision 2, self-pity was labeled as the silent assassin that kills our potential and ability to control our Response. It holds us hostage to the whims of what Event may befall us.

Instead of giving in to the anxiety and stress, take control of it. Take away its power to overcome your thoughts.

During his time as emperor, Marcus Aurelius kept a series of writings, but it appears Aurelius never intended for the writings to be published. Rather, they were words of wisdom or advice to himself, which he often made while he was planning military campaigns. The work has survived the centuries and is widely referred to simply as the *Meditations*.

Aurelius's writings are broken into twelve books (or chapters). In the third book, Aurelius wrote:

> *Your ability to control your thoughts—treat it with respect. It's all that protects your mind from false perceptions—false to your nature, and that of all rational beings. It's what makes thoughtfulness possible, and affection for other people, and submission to the divine.*[64]

The mind of the Stoic works to separate itself from emotion. Emotion is important, and we should not try to escape it. That is a different problem. However, emotion without rational thought and without logical analysis is a poor decision maker. There is incredible power in taking an Event and working hard to see it for what it is dispassionately. To analyze it from all angles without the filter of your emotion or biases. Once analyzed in that way, our emotions then inform us and should not be completely dismissed in our decision-making. It is important, however, to understand how our emotions affect our thoughts and perceptions.

Another important tenet of Stoic philosophy is to learn which things are controllable, which are not, and to treat each accordingly. With our football players, I try to teach them to "control the controllables." That means to obsess and worry about the things you can control, but not the things you cannot. A player can control the process of preparation, but they do not have total control over the outcome of the contest. I ask the players to focus on their process to prepare for the game—know the game plan, the opponent, do the necessary work to be fully prepared mentally, emotionally, and physically, and to play at their best. This gives us the greatest opportunity to experience success in the contest.

However, things will happen that affect the outcome we cannot control. The weather can be bad. Injuries can strike. The official's calls may go against us. The opponent may play better than we do, and the ball may not bounce our way.

Epictetus wrote: "Things in our control are opinion, pursuit, desire, aversion, and, in a word, whatever are our own actions. Things not in our control are body, property, reputation, command, and, in a word, whatever are not our own actions."[65]

Resilience is learning how to become comfortable with some things being outside our control. Similarly, learning to apply ourselves in those areas where we have control is equally important to our resilience. In the **E + R = O** model, we cannot control the Event, but we can control the

Response. We can choose to be defined by how we respond to the Events of life.

When we can become stoic with Events, when we can analyze them dispassionately and can chart a Response objectively without the filter of our emotion, then we maximize our ability for successful Outcomes.

Processing life's Events through a stoic lens, or better yet a grateful lens, does not mean denying negativity or reality. It is not a form of superficial or fake happiness. Instead, it means realizing the power you possess to transform an obstacle into an opportunity. It means reframing a loss into a potential gain and recasting negativity into positive channels for gratitude.

In a study conducted at Eastern Washington University, participants were randomly assigned to one of three writing groups that would recall and report on an unpleasant memory—a loss, betrayal, victimization, or some other personally upsetting experience.[66] The first group wrote for twenty minutes on issues irrelevant to their unpleasant memory. The second group wrote about their experience pertaining to their unpleasant memory. The third group focused on the positive aspects of the unpleasant memory and, with the benefit of perspective, what about that difficult experience might now make them feel grateful.

Results showed that the third group demonstrated more closure and less unpleasant emotional impact. Participants in the study were never told to ignore the negative aspects of the experience or to deny the pain and unpleasantness. Moreover, participants who found reasons to be grateful became less focused on debilitating questions and emotions, such as why the bad event happened, whether the bad event could have been prevented, or if they believed they caused the bad event to happen. [67] This study validates personal experience that finding the good in an unpleasant experience can help heal troubling memories and, in a sense, redeem them.

THE PRISONER

During the time of Seneca, while Epictetus was a boy and before the birth of Marcus Aurelius, a Roman citizen with Jewish heritage grew up in the town of Tarsus, still located in modern-day Turkey. In Hebrew, his name was Saul, likely named after the first appointed king of Israel. He is most widely remembered today by his Latin name, Paul. Paul's letters to various churches or church leaders comprise almost half of the books of the modern Bible's New Testament. Paul's life was not easy. His story is summarized below to put into context the wisdom he shared about facing adversity.

Paul grew up in a household with strict religious beliefs. At a young age, he was sent to another city (Jerusalem) to study under the noted rabbi, Gamaliel. Paul was a self-admitted religious zealot.[68] In fact, he first appears in the Bible executing one of the early converts to Christianity named Stephen.

Paul experienced a miraculous conversion when Jesus appeared and spoke to him through a light from heaven. Paul was blinded and led into the city of Damascus where he met with a respected Jewish man, Ananias, who had converted to Christianity. Ananias laid hands on Paul and restored his sight. Paul came to believe in this new Christian way, the very thing he had so passionately opposed.

Shortly after his conversion, he narrowly eluded death in Damascus at the hands of the city's governor. He escaped through a window in the city's wall by being lowered by a basket. Then, with the same passion with which he had opposed the Christian way, Paul supported it and traveled throughout the ancient world preaching about the faith he had adopted. In his travels, he was met with continual, constant, and life-threatening resistance. In a letter to the Church in Corinth, Paul wrote:

> *Five times I have received from the Jews the forty lashes minus one. Three times I was beaten with rods, once I was stoned, three times I was shipwrecked, I spent a night and a day in open sea, I have been constantly on the move. I have been in danger from rivers, in danger from bandits, in danger from my own countrymen, in danger from Gentiles; in danger in the city, in danger in the country, in danger at sea; and in danger from false brothers. I have labored and toiled and have often gone without sleep; I have known hunger and thirst and have often gone without food; I have been cold and naked.*[69]

After returning from his travels to his adopted home city of Jerusalem, a group of "Jews from Asia" who opposed Paul began to stir up opposition against him.[70] Soon, there was an uproar in the city against Paul. A mob seized him, dragged him into the Jewish temple in Jerusalem, and tried to kill him. The Roman authorities rushed in and arrested Paul.

While the local Roman authorities were investigating his case, a group plotted to kill Paul while he was being transported for questioning. So, the local authority gathered a large armed contingent to transport Paul under cover of darkness to a regional authority (the governor). He was held under house arrest for two years. After a leadership change, the new governor gave Paul a hearing and was inclined to send him back to Jerusalem for trial.

Paul, perhaps knowing a trial in Jerusalem would likely result in him being ambushed and killed before he ever arrived, petitioned to be heard by the Roman Emperor. The authorities then placed Paul on a boat bound for Rome to meet with the Emperor.

The trip to Rome, however, was fraught with disaster. The ship ran into a fierce storm and eventually ran aground at the isle of Malta. Paul and his jailers stayed on Malta for three months before again leaving for Rome. Upon arrival in Rome, he was placed under house arrest for two years while waiting to see the Emperor. History leaves us wondering about what happened next, although some historians record that Paul was beheaded by order of the Emperor Nero.

For the person wrestling with adversity, there is much to learn from Paul. Paul did not let his adversity take him off-mission. He demonstrated incredible perseverance. Though steeped in hardship, he shared his witness with other prisoners, his jailers, and even the authorities deciding his case. During the imprisonment in Rome, Paul is believed to have written four letters that made their way into our modern Bible—Ephesians (a letter to the Church in Ephesus), Philippians (a letter to the Church in Philippi), Colossians (a letter to the Church in Colossae), and Philemon (a letter written to an individual living in Colossae). The thoughts of Paul, while imprisoned for no justifiable reason, give wise counsel on how to be resilient in adversity.

First, Paul was very focused on his Response to the Events that happened to him. He wrote that his imprisonment allowed him to further his mission because it gave him a chance to share his witness with the palace guard.[71] This was an influential audience that he likely never would have met if not for his imprisonment. Paul found reasons to be grateful for his difficult circumstance. He did not dwell on why bad Events happened to him or who was to blame for them.

Second, Paul shared his thoughts concerning mindset. Having spent years in confinement, at times with his life at risk, Paul must have wrestled with staying in a productive frame of mind. He shared this: "Whatever is true, whatever is noble, whatever is right, whatever is pure, whatever is lovely, whatever admirable–if anything is excellent or praise-worthy–think about such things."[72]

Third, Paul learned to be comfortable with things he could not control. He wrote: "I know what it is to be in need, and I know what it is to have plenty. I have learned the secret of being content in any and every situation, whether well fed or hungry, whether living in plenty or in want. I can do all this through him who gives me strength."[73]

Even when in incredible adversity, confined for no reason and navigating threats on his life, Paul demonstrated the tools of the resilient. Though you may not suffer physical confinement, you may feel confined by circumstances or impediments beyond your control. Though you may not face an angry mob looking to execute you, you may feel as though the world is against you and out to get you. When navigating difficult times, remember Paul's wisdom. Find a reason to be grateful. Meditate on the true, the noble, the right, the pure, the lovely, and the things that are excellent and praiseworthy. Find contentment in the circumstance you are in—whether in need or in plenty.

The reality of your circumstance is governed by the frame through which you see it. The farmer would look at a bad Event and say: "Who knows? We shall see." The Stoic would look at a bad Event and say: "Your worry about an Event comes only because of the emotion you allow yourself to assign to it." Paul would say: ". . . we also rejoice in our sufferings, because we know that suffering produces perseverance; perseverance [produces] character; and character [produces] hope. And hope does not disappoint us, because God has poured his love into our hearts . . ."[74]

So, now the questions come to you: *Through which frame will you view your circumstance? Will you find good in it? What emotions will you allow yourself to assign to an Event? Will the Event control you? Or will you apply a Response to that Event that leads to a positive Outcome?*

DECISION 8
DECIDE TO CREATE A RESILIENT INTERNAL SCRIPT

THE SOUNDTRACK IN YOUR MIND

W e say thousands of words to ourselves every hour we are awake, constantly creating a story that is the lens through which we see the world around us and through which we see ourselves. This story holds incredible power over us.

Think for a moment about your favorite movie. The one you have seen four or five (or more) times. One of my favorite movies is *While You Were Sleeping*. The movie features Sandra Bullock and Bill Pullman and tells the story of a Chicago Transit Authority worker who has a chance encounter with a handsome commuter. The plot of *While You Were Sleeping* quickly unfolds during the week between Christmas and New Year's Day. Watching it is one of our family traditions on Christmas Eve. While it is on, we can often finish the actors' lines. Sometimes, we recite lines from the movie to each other in funny situations that arise at other times of the year. We know the dialogue from that movie, and our subconscious can call it up with little prompting.

You probably also have a movie or movies where the lines pop into your mind with the right stimulus. Now, imagine that same power multiplied many times over with the story we have playing in our heads. We hear that internal script playing all the time, not only once a year on Christmas Eve.

> "IF YOU THINK YOU CAN, YOU CAN. IF YOU THINK YOU CAN'T, YOU CAN'T."—DEL HOWARD, MANAGER OF THE SAN FRANCISCO SEALS BASEBALL CLUB (1914)[75]

If our internal script says, "*I am not good enough. I can't do that. Who am I to try this?*" Those limitations become a self-fulfilling reality.

Now consider a script playing in our mind that says, "*I can do this. I am worthy. I have what it takes.*" Such a script will not bring activity and success by itself, but it is a critical first step to create a foundational belief for success. That foundational belief is a necessary part of our motivation to act. We are more likely to start something when we believe it will be successful.

"I AM"

The most powerful word in any language is the word that follows "*I am . . .*" In the game of football, the big guys up front, the offensive linemen, protect the quarterback and make lanes for the running backs. Offensive linemen, particularly in junior high and high school, are generally not the best athletes on the team. They are not the fastest, most agile, most graceful, nor are they typically the first ones invited to the Sadie Hawkins dances.

As a result, offensive linemen often suffer from bruised self-esteem. They see themselves as inferior to their more athletic teammates. They often spend their entire lives feeling like the last ones picked for a team on the playground.

As their coach, it is important to infuse confidence and belief into these players. I tell them to control with intention the two words in their minds that follow "*I am.*"

I paste this sign into their lockers:

I AM . . .
STRONG
EQUIPPED
CONFIDENT
MORE THAN A CONQUEROR

Playing offensive line is hard. It is a one-on-one battle against the same player who lines up twelve to eighteen inches away from them throughout the game. For seventy to eighty plays, an offensive lineman tries to win each play and competition. It is a physical, mental, and psychological battle.

If an offensive lineman ever begins to believe he is insufficient to win those individual contests, it is going to be a long night. They must go into each play believing they have a plan and the physical ability to win the play.

When in the heat of battle, we revert to our training, and when the stress of competition sets in, the player's subconscious thoughts and muscle memory take over. Thus, it is imperative for their mental script and subconscious thoughts to tell them a story that provides them with a solid foundation for success.

The same is true for any of us in the thousands of small decisions we make during the day. *Will we wake up when planned or will we sleep in?* If we have convinced ourselves we will have a successful day and are disciplined to follow through with our plans, we are more likely to wake up as planned. *Will we speak up at the meeting and share our ideas? Or will we remain silent?* If we believe we are worthy and our ideas have value, we are far more likely to speak up.

Resilient people are intentional about the script playing in their mind. Consistent positive beliefs become positive actions when we believe things like: *I am an overcomer. I am worthy. I am successful. I am loved.*

How Do We Create a Resilient Internal Story?

Creating an internal story that leads to resilient and winning choices starts with being intentional with the words you say to yourself. In May 2020, Elon Musk, during an interview on *The Joe Rogan Podcast,* predicted that, with the help of brain implant devices, humans would be able to communicate nonverbally within the decade of the 2020s.

Musk was asked, ". . . one day in the future there's going to come a time where you can read each other's minds and you'll be able to interface with each other in some sort of a nonverbal, non-physical way where you will transfer data back and forth to each other without having to actually use your mouth?"

"Yeah, exactly," Musk responded.[76]

As I started to imagine that possibility, I considered all those unspoken thoughts I have and wondered if people would *hear* those thoughts too? When I am thinking, *this guy is boring me,* will he hear that? Or *I don't know if I trust this person.* Or *Wow, this person's voice is really annoying.* How about when I hold back some information that I do not wish to disclose? Will someone connected to my brain frequency be able to read those thoughts? The implications are immense.

However, in a way, this technology already exists. It is just limited to you hearing your own unspoken thoughts. You do not have to speak aloud to know and hear what you are saying to yourself—your internal story. Now, consider this: If someone you did not know spoke to you the way you speak to yourself, what would you do? For many, if someone spoke to us like we speak to ourselves, you might slug them, return with a few choice words, or give them a nasty look.

So, stop. Stop the script. Stop the negative words. Interrupt the thought pattern. Create a winning script. Determine what you want your internal script to be and take it to heart. When the negative script starts, interrupt it.

To do this, you must really internalize the positive script. It is easy to let our positive attributes slip from the mind. This is particularly true when our internal practice of intentionally recognizing our positive traits has not been well ingrained.

Running a positive script is like muscle memory. When a muscle is trained to do something repeatedly (like throwing a ball or signing your name), you can do it with minimal thought. It just happens with repetitive internalization. To get that repetitive internalization, you must be intentional about creating that tract in your mind.

STRATEGY #1 FOR CREATING A RESILIENT INTERNAL SCRIPT: REPEAT AN IDEA ROUTINELY

One strategy for intentionally creating an internal script is to repeat something to yourself routinely—either daily or twice a day—that you want to embody as you live life each day. You can have a saying (such as, "I am capable," "I will succeed," and "I am a good father") written on a notecard stuck to your mirror. You can turn the saying (or affirmation) into a screen saver. I have a PowerPoint file I review each morning with twelve to fifteen slides of thoughts, goals, or affirmations I want to keep top of mind. I keep the PowerPoint on all my devices—phone, tablet, computer—so I always have access to it. There is a master copy stored in the cloud (Dropbox) that I can pull down to any of my devices each time I update or change what is in the PowerPoint.

Daniel Kahneman won the 2002 Nobel Prize in Economics and is the author of a best-selling and impactful book called *Thinking, Fast and Slow*. In it, Kahneman posits that the words we speak to ourselves do not yet even need to be provable to be impactful. "[A] message, unless it is immediately rejected as a lie, will have the same effect on the associative system regardless of its reliability . . . Whether the story is true, or believable, matters little, if at all."[77] The story that we tell ourselves about ourselves—whether right or wrong—becomes our story.

Muhammad Ali was the greatest boxer of a generation. There were several characteristics that led to his success, but one of his key attributes was an unfailing belief in himself. He began calling himself "the greatest" before he became a champion. Ali was set to fight Sonny Liston for the heavyweight belt. Ali was a 7-1 underdog. Nonetheless, in a televised interview leading up to the fight, Ali proclaimed, "I am the greatest." He went on to beat Liston and won the title.

Ali is a practical illustration of the inherent power in our thought life. He said: "It's the repetition of affirmation

> IT'S THE REPETITION OF AFFIRMATION THAT LEADS TO BELIEF, AND ONCE THAT BELIEF BECOMES A DEEP CONVICTION, THINGS BEGIN TO HAPPEN. — MUHAMMED ALI (2012)

that leads to belief, and once that belief becomes a deep conviction, things begin to happen."[78] Ali had belief before he had believers.

Strategy #2 for Creating a Resilient Internal Script: Play a Mental Movie

Another effective strategy for creating a resilient internal script is visualization. For me (and many others), having a picture or image in my mind of who I am and where I want to be is powerful. Just as it is important to be intentional about the script running through our minds, it is important to be intentional about the mental images and pictures—the mental movies—that play in our heads. There is great power in creating pictures and movies in our minds of what we want to be and do.

I keep a vision board next to the desk at my office. The vision board has sayings, life dreams, a list of people I want to keep in the front of my mind and pray over, images of things I desire, and the images of things I have accomplished. Keeping this board where I can see it often keeps things in my mind that might otherwise slip away in the day-to-day routine of life.

Everything that was ever created or achieved first started as an idea in someone's mind. The idea was likely generated in response to a need or desire, and the idea took hold. The person focused mental energy on it, and it built upon itself as the mental energy became infused with emotions. The combination of the idea, the mental energy, and the emotion created a deep desire, and the person's mind went into overdrive looking for ways to marry the vision with physical reality.

This phenomenon is often called confirmation bias or, more academically, the Baader-Meinhof phenomenon. This occurs when someone stumbles upon a unique piece of information—often an unfamiliar word or name—and soon afterward, encounters the same subject again, often repeatedly. You might have experienced this when you last bought a car. When you are thinking about buying or have purchased a certain make or model of car, you begin to see that make or model everywhere. You notice it far more than you ever had before.

The same is true for what you think about in other arenas of life. You will notice and gravitate toward what you hold in your mind and visualize.

At times, I have resisted using affirmations and visualizations. It felt countercultural, out of the norm, and uncomfortably weird. However, to rise above our natural gravitation toward our comfort zone, a key tool is to visualize doing something greater, grander, more impactful.

Elite athletes do this all the time. They visualize themselves flawlessly executing a complex, difficult, and strenuous physical action. This vision of perfection has physical consequences. In 2015, the U.S. Women's Soccer Team beat Japan in the final of the World Cup led by one of its stars, Carli Lloyd. In an interview after the final game, Ms. Lloyd said she used visualization to see herself being successful on the field. Before the 2015 final, she prepared and then played a mind movie of scoring four goals. She ended up scoring three in a 5-2 victory. "When you're feeling good mentally and physically, those plays are just instincts," Lloyd said. "It just happens."[79]

In the early 1990s, Jim Carrey, now known for his roles in numerous blockbuster movies, was an unknown and struggling actor. In an effort to rise above the adversity, he wrote himself a check for $10 million for "acting services rendered," dated it for 1994, and carried it in his wallet for inspiration. Carrey earned exactly $10 million for his role in *Dumb and Dumber* . . . in 1994. Carrey went on to be one of America's highest-earning movie stars, and he credits visualization with helping him get there.[80]

Kerri Walsh Jennings and Misty May-Treanor are the most successful female beach volleyball team in history. They entered four Olympics and won three gold medals and one bronze. In an interview during their preparation for the

2016 Summer Olympics, Jennings said: "A lot of what we do is visualization. To be able to ... take in the sights, the sounds, the stress, the excitement, that's going to serve us really well moving forward."[81]

Even as a young athlete, Arnold Schwarzenegger used the power of visualization to reach his goals and become a world-class bodybuilder. He would look at the champions in the magazines. He fixated on one of them named Reg Park. "His image was my ideal. It was fixed indelibly in my mind . . . he was the image in front of me from the time I started training. The more I focused in on this image and worked and grew, the more I saw it was real and possible for me to be like him."[82] Later, when he transitioned to careers in acting and politics, Schwarzenegger said he employed similar mental images: "It's the same process I used in bodybuilding: What you do is create a vision of who you want to be—and then live that picture as if it were already true."[83]

Lindsey Vonn is one of the most successful female skiers in history. She won a gold medal in the 2010 Winter Olympics and five overall World Cup Championships. Before leaving on a run, Vonn closed her eyes at the start gate and swayed from side to side, running through the course in her mind. "I always visualize the run before I do it. By the time I get to the start gate, I've run the course 100 times already in my head, picturing how I'll take the turns."[84]

In fact, well before race day, Vonn visualized key races. Months before the 2010 Vancouver Games, Vonn was in a workout room at a training center in Salzburg, Austria. She balanced each foot on a nylon slackline suspended three feet off the rubber floor and visualized flying through the course while crouched in an aerodynamic tuck, hands clenched in front of her chin as if holding her poles. Her trainer enhanced the picture in her mind by speaking gently into her right ear: "You're on the downhill course at Whistler (the Olympic venue). . . ." Vonn closed her eyes and shifted her weight rhythmically from one foot to the other as if executing high-speed turns on a Canadian mountainside more than 5,000 miles and many months away. She took forceful, deep breaths to simulate the aerobic demands of being on the course.

"I love that exercise," says Vonn. "Once I visualize a course, I never forget it. So I get on those lines and go through exactly the run that I want to have. I control my emotions and just make it routine."[85]

Visualization is not just for elite athletes or actors, however. Recently, I had a legal hearing in front of three judges on a court of appeals panel. The hearing would take place via teleconference using Zoom. In the weeks leading up to the event, I did two rehearsals to mock panels of other lawyers that I asked to help simulate the real argument. I researched what my computer screen would look like while delivering my argument to the court. Then, in the days leading up to the hearing, I spent a few minutes each day visualizing how everything would look, where I would stare into the camera, and what I was going to say. On the morning before the hearing, I did it all again. I was far more confident and relaxed in the moment because of the preparation via visualization.

Do you need to have a critical conversation? See it in your mind and play through it first. Do you have an important meeting at work? Create a mental movie of where it is going to happen, where everyone will be, how you want to appear, and what you want to say. Is there an area of life where you want to see change? Picture your life in that changed state. Want to be thinner? Create a mental picture of a thinner you and figure out what it will take to get there. Infuse emotion into your mental picture to drive action. Why do you want to be thinner? What joy does it bring? What pain comes from not being thinner? What are you giving up? What health consequences are you creating? Do you really feel the pain from those consequences? Visualize those and experience them at an emotional level.

Use the Baader-Meinhof phenomena to your advantage. Visualize where you want to be and what you want to do. Then, let your mind see the things, make the connections, and grab the ideas to take you from mental picture to reality.

STRATEGY #3 FOR CREATING A RESILIENT INTERNAL SCRIPT: BE INTENTIONAL ABOUT YOUR INTAKE

A third strategy for feeding the positive is to be mindful about what content you consume. What do you watch and listen to? Is it advancing your life or only passing your time?

Well-known motivational speaker, Zig Ziglar, used to talk about "Automobile University." The concept is to turn drive time into learning time. It refers to redeeming what might otherwise be inefficient time into opportunities to feed your mind. If you spend time in a car, bus, or train, turn off the radio and put on a book or podcast. On a piece of exercise equipment, you can train your body and your mind at the same time. Often, I wear headphones and listen while washing the dishes or folding clothes. I call it "cleaning house and cleaning my mind." Undoubtedly, you have time you could use to either absorb content that will positively affect the script in your mind or to learn new things that will advance your life.

When significant resistance arrives—failure, adversities, conflict—it is imperative to have a positive script running in your mind to overcome and get past the resistance trying to stop your progress or set you back.

Just as important as being intentional about what you listen to, is being intentional about who you listen to. The maxim that you become the average of the five people you associate with the most carries truth. Be careful spending time around negative people who wallow in their problems and fail to focus on solutions. Often, they want people to join them in their misery and pity. This allows them to feel better about themselves. They can justify their inability to solve problems by the others they can convince to be equally helpless.

ASSOCIATE WITH THOSE WHO WILL MAKE A BETTER [VERSION] OF YOU.—SENECA (63 B.C.)[86]

I can feel pressure to listen to negative people because I do not want to be thought of as callous, rude, or dismissive. Maybe you have felt the same way. There is a fine line between lending a sympathetic ear to someone and getting sucked into their negative emotional spiral. Resilient people avoid getting drawn in. They set limits and build moats between themselves and negative people when necessary.

In the middle of 2020, people became very aware of the airborne transmission of a virus. A cough or sneeze sounded like a siren and turned people's heads to investigate whether that person's mouth was covered or if they looked sick. The health authorities suggested everyone should wear a mask when out in public.

Negativity also spreads like a virus, from person to person. One person's negative thoughts shared with another begin to take root in their mind. Guard yourself and stay away from it when you can. When someone does spew negativity or verbal attacks, a strong immune system can keep you upright.

Your cognitive immune system is the internal script playing in your mind. When it is positive and uplifting, you can better withstand the negativity and verbal attacks. Take these three steps—repeat an idea routinely, play a mental movie, and be intentional about your intake—and watch your mood, attitude, and resistance rise.

DECISION 9
DECIDE TO REMEMBER WHO YOU ARE

THE SIGN ON YOUR DOOR

Bill Mead spent a lifetime serving others—his family, his country, his church. Born into poverty, he worked hard, got an education, joined the Navy, and later became a minister. When he was diagnosed with dementia, his family made the difficult decision to place him in specialized care.

However, Mead's lack of memory did not change his story or how unique he is. Mead's son, Patrick, was determined to make sure his dad would not become another patient in a memory care facility. Patrick said, "My fear was here's this man among strangers, they don't know him. They don't understand who he is, and he can't tell them. So, I wrote just

> TAKING CONTROL OF YOUR ATTITUDE AND CONFIDENCE LEVEL IS ONE OF THE MOST POWERFUL THINGS YOU CAN DO TO INFLUENCE YOUR SUCCESS, YOUR FAILURE, AND YOUR ABILITY TO OVERCOME SETBACKS.

a short set of sentences and we had it posted on his door."[87]
The note said:

My name is Bill Mead.
I was born in abject poverty.
I became a warrior (US Navy, Korea War era).
I then laid aside my weapons and
Became a minister and missionary.
I traveled the world, spreading the
Gospel of Jesus Christ,
Bringing hope, medicine, and love
To the United States, Europe,
South America and Africa.
I am slowly leaving this earth
For my heavenly home.
This may take awhile.
Thank you for remembering who I was.
And who I am.
I am a man, a warrior, a missionary,
A father, a friend, and much more.
And I have one more river to cross.[88]

Patrick Mead's love for his Dad is touching, and the note left on Bill Mead's door is a helpful reminder that each of us has a story. We are all unique and have value.

However, like Bill Mead, we often forget our story, our uniqueness, our value. We may not suffer from dementia, but we forget because adversity clouds our memory; voices in our ears or in our heads tell us the untrue story that we lack value or resilience. Sometimes, we drift away and forget who we are, that we have overcome adversities in life and can do so again. When we forget our story, core values, unique talents, and abilities, we allow ourselves to stray off course. We forget the victories we have fought and won. We forget the abilities we have shown to overcome adversities.

An athlete or team riding a winning streak plays with extreme confidence. Even while bad things are happening in a game or contest, they believe they can overcome and win. This belief is buoyed by the string of wins in their immediate past and present conscience.

I have coached teams who, pre-game, believed they were going to win and others who believed they were going to lose. There is a different mentality, energy, and posture in how they stand and move. Their belief in whether they will win or lose often is a self-fulfilling prophecy.

Undoubtedly, there are obstacles you have already successfully navigated—difficult times in school, relationships that broke apart, times you did not get the job or the promotion. Nonetheless, you withstood.

The adversity may be bigger and scarier than any others you have previously faced in the past. It may be a larger unknown. It may have a less clear future, but your memory of your past success will fuel and challenge the next big obstacle.

* * *

Don English watched the 2016 World Series with great interest. Coach English is one of the most successful high school baseball coaches in Texas history. Before he retired after the 2019 season, his teams won 663 games over a thirty-seven-year career. However, in the 2016 World Series, he got a rare treat. The classic series was an intense matchup between the Chicago Cubs and Cleveland Indians. In this best four out of seven series, the teams split the first six games. The decisive Game Seven went into extra innings with the Cubs winning the final game 8-7 and ending the longest World Series drought in Major League Baseball history.

As compelling as the series and the Cubs storyline were, Coach English watched with an even greater special interest. Two pitchers he coached in high school were standouts in the Series—Corey Kluber for the Cubs and Jake Arrieta for the Indians. In five of the seven World Series games, one of his former players was a starting pitcher. Kluber started game one. Arrieta started game two. Kluber started game four. Arrieta started game six. Kluber started game seven.

Kluber and Arrieta were not the only players English coached who had professional careers. Between the number of high school wins and the players who went on to success in baseball and other professions, this was a career marked with success and achievement. However, Coach English also had his share of setbacks. One of them almost derailed him.

In 2002, English was hired for the head baseball job at a high school in an affluent Dallas suburb. By most measures, he was successful. Over his nine years, his teams went 211-106-1 and made the playoffs eight times. Those playoff runs included two appearances in both the regional quarterfinals and semifinals.

Coach English's teams were not solely defined by wins and losses, however. He did what we hope coaches will do—he created a positive team environment, taught his players life lessons that transcended baseball, and modeled a life worth living. After a playoff exit in 2009, he was taken to task on a Texas high school baseball blog. The parent of a player on the team posted this in defense of Coach English: "It is not Coach English's fault, he cannot lay down bunts, catch flies, field grounders or hit for our players. He can encourage, lead a life of integrity worth being imitated and love these players like his own sons, which he has done for almost 30 years."[89]

Despite managing what most would consider an enviable program, English had detractors. This is not unusual in the coaching profession, where it is impossible to please everyone and success brings only higher expectations. However, English's detractors were influential in a relatively tight-knit community. During his nine years at this school, the mayor's son and the son of the head of the local youth baseball association tried out for English's teams. Neither player had the talent to make the team, and both were cut. These are the kinds of hard choices coaches often must make. It can generate hard feelings and can be exceedingly tough when those feelings belong to people with an outsized voice.

English's squad went 30-8-1 in 2011, but he was dismissed after his team lost in the second round of the playoffs. Unfortunately, English was not just dismissed. Certain people in the community, always anonymous, tried to make his life miserable. One day, he found a For Sale sign in his front yard. Another day, after not receiving mail for several days, he found out someone had filed a fake change of address form with the post office, and his mail was being forwarded to a different city. On other days, adult magazines arrived at the house addressed to his wife after someone had taken out subscriptions in her name. Blistering posts were made on websites that reached the local baseball community.

Generally, coaches are not dismissed when they have the success that English's program had experienced. So, naturally, everyone assumed English must have been dismissed because of inappropriate or bad conduct. Coach English described it this way: "People thought I had done something wrong or I wouldn't be leaving . . . a coach looks at what I had going and assumed 'he'd only [be dismissed] for one reason. He got in trouble. He did something immoral or unethical.'"[90]

After experiencing tremendous success and then having it all ripped away unfairly, how do you bounce back? How do you find your second wind? How do you keep from becoming bitter? When reflecting on the experience many years later, Coach English shared something profound:

> It's in our DNA to just fight and keep on fighting. To put your head down and fight. Fight for the right to be right. Then, to think, all that time, God was trying to tell me and then

finally taught me—it's not about being right. It's about being the right man. I coach to influence kids. As things got more difficult, it caused me to go deeper into my higher purpose.[91]

Coach English, with the help of the Lord's influence, retained a focus on why he was doing what he was doing. He remembered who he was and what he wanted to be about. He remembered his higher purpose: "I coach to influence kids." Amid the adversity, unfairness, and the threat to his career and livelihood, it would have been easy to walk away feeling unappreciated and soured. However, as he gave up fighting for the right to be right and the natural concern we all have for what people think and believe about us, his ability to keep moving forward was propelled by remembering who he was.

You have an innate ability to conquer obstacles because you have done it before and can do it again. This opponent may differ from those of the past, but you have won before and you can win again. We need to remember who we are and what we have done.

Another important reason to remember who we are is because the adversities of life—whether large or small—can easily take us off our chosen path. We get complacent with where are, even if it is not where we thought we would be or should be. Internally, however, we know we are off course. We feel a sense of discomfort, a little voice telling us we are off track. That discomfort is our internal GPS nudging us. It is like the map on our smartphone saying, "Return to course." When you feel the discomfort or hear the voice telling you that you are off track, do not ignore or bury it. It is telling you something of value. Hear it and heed it.

Remember who you are and the seeds of greatness within you. Course-correct as needed. Resume your journey on the path that is yours.

When Patrick Mead pinned his dad's story to the door, he created a powerful vision for each person who entered Bill Mead's room. I encourage you to do the same thing for yourself. Write out a few sentences of who you are, who you have been, and where you want to be. Pin it somewhere you will see it as a reminder. Even if we do not suffer from memory loss, we often forget who we are and where we are headed.

Even in the midst of losing his job and the swirl of voices criticizing him, Coach English heard his internal GPS reminding him of his purpose—to "be the right man" and to coach "to influence kids." That vision of who he was and who he was supposed to be allowed him to overcome the obstacles hurled into his path.

REMEMBERING PAST SUCCESSES

One way we build confidence in what we can achieve in the future is to remember our past successes. This is a virtuous cycle.

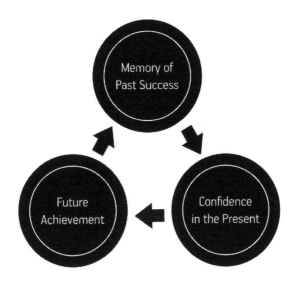

When we reflect on past success, we reinforce our confidence that we can experience success in the future. I have often heard the advice to not look back, but to focus on the future. That is true to an extent. However, acknowledging and remembering past successes is an important part of motivation. Sustaining or recovering motivation is an important part of resilience.

You may have heard the phrase, "If you can believe it, you can achieve it." This is an oft-quoted adaption of Napoleon Hill's phrase in his book, *Think and Grow Rich.* In describing Thomas Edison, Hill says that Edison "knew that the mind could produce anything the mind could conceive and believe . . . ."[92] Although some may doubt the value of the thought as positive psychology snake oil, I have seen and experienced its truth. Equally true is its corollary: If you do not believe you can achieve it, you are right.

A belief in one's ability to achieve a result is called "self-efficacy" by psychologists.[93] A robust sense of self-efficacy leads to high motivation. When we believe in our ability, we are far more likely to put in the work to achieve the success. Sustaining motivation toward an objective is a large determinant in whether we are successful in reaching that objective.

Reflecting on our past successes will build self-efficacy. It will reinforce our belief that we have what it takes to be successful and give us the fuel to keep striving and finding motivation in the challenges.

Perhaps you are facing something larger than you have ever faced before. You may feel uncertainty about whether you can tackle an obstacle so large. However, small wins lead to bigger wins. Search out what it will take to overcome the larger challenge. Can you do small things to move you closer to overcoming? Have you done similar things in the past?

For many years, I served as the hiring partner for an international law firm. As part of that role, I interviewed hundreds of law students vying for jobs. These were students at the top of their classes from the best schools in the country. They were very smart and well-polished. Their resumes were impressive. As an interviewer, my job was to get behind the resume and see through the very polished exterior to uncover the real person sitting in front of me. One question I almost always asked was: "What have you done in your life that you are the proudest of?"

In most cases, that question pierced through the well-constructed exterior to the person's emotional center. Sometimes, they thought about their answer, but other times, it came to them quickly. However, it almost always evoked an emotional response as they relived a moment when they experienced victory.

Think about that question for a moment. *What have you done in your life that you are the proudest of?* Whatever memory it evoked, you were impressive. You exhibited the tools for success and showed the world you had what it took. Bottle that up. That is self-efficacy. That memory will drive your future success. You can do it. When you carry that belief, it provides motivation to keep going, and that is the fuel you will need for making the journey.

Decision 10

DECIDE TO FOCUS ON YOUR STRENGTHS

Claiming the Treasure

The best football coaches can mold their game plan to what their players do well. They do things in their schemes to optimize their players' ability to be successful. Not the biggest team? Then emphasize and take advantage of your team speed. Not the biggest or the fastest team? Hopefully, your players are aggressive or smart, and you can adapt your schemes and strategies to take advantage of the assets you have.

The same is true for you. There are things you do well—your superpowers. But for the things you do not do well, where do you focus your attention? When we are in adversity, it is easy to focus on our shortcomings. We get myopic on areas where we struggle. However, what if we focused on our strengths and adapted so our strengths could elevate us above the adversity?

Anyone can look around and find others who appear better, smarter, more talented, and more attractive than we are. These feelings of lack can be an obstacle to our resiliency.

They require a mindset change. Instead of focusing on where you fall short, focus on what you have.

Cateura is a community built on the landfill on the outskirts of Asuncion, the capital city of Paraguay. Most people in this impoverished area make their living by selling plastic bottles or anything they can recycle from the garbage. The community is surrounded by trash, poverty, and lack of education. The environment is toxic for its inhabitants, especially children and young people who are prone to delinquency and drugs.

However, since 2006, a light of hope has arisen in Cateura. A group of children perform in the Recycled Orchestra. The instruments are made with materials found in the trash. Old water pipes become saxophones. Forks, knives, spoons, and coins become the keys. Cans and bake trays are used to make violins. Percussion drums are made with wooden pallets or trash cans.

One of the founders, Favio Chavez, an environmental technician and music teacher, describes the Recycled Orchestra this way: "This is a social project that uses music as a catalyst. We are working intensively with many families and many children. We propose a life change, projected into the future. This is a mission. I feel God's presence. I believe things happen according to His plans."[94]

This mission was also possible thanks to the help of Nicolás Gómez, a trash picker turned into an instrument craftsman. From the beginning, he was in charge of finding the materials to manufacture the musical instruments. According to Gómez, "Garbage is not garbage. If you have creative ideas, you can do anything with garbage."[95]

"I think we have to be grateful for the gifts we have received," added Chávez. "We must be responsible because those gifts should serve others, too. It's like what the Bible says: You can't hide a light under the table. The light has to be where it can illuminate everyone."[96]

This humble orchestra is illuminating Cateura. The village has become the subject of renown due to the 2015 documentary film *Landfill Harmonic*. The Recycled Orchestra has been invited to perform concerts worldwide with musicians as varied as Stevie Wonder, Metallica, and Megadeath. The orchestra has received awards from the Royal Crowns of the Netherlands and Spain. Favio Chávez and the children of Cateura have given lectures at the famous TED conferences and have inspired millions.

Andrés Riveros spent many of his formative adult years in the orchestra. He traveled to more than twenty countries for the concerts, but he dreams of staying in Cateura the rest of his life to transform it and make it a model community. "Some people are born with everything. Others are not," he continued. "But everyone has to make progress in their own way. This is ours, with music, with recycling. Maybe we are changing part of our society and the mentality of our own people."[97] Based on the success of the Recycled Orchestra, similar organizations were formed in Brazil, Burundi, Ecuador, Mexico, Panama, and Spain.

You have talents and abilities that can help you rise above whatever adversity is weighing on you. In fact, you have talents and abilities that can change the world around you in a positive way. You may not recognize them as such. You may see limitations, deficits, or trash. However, trash can be transformed into an instrument that can play beautiful music. It starts with what you see.

* * *

Superman's identity was always Superman. Even when he took off the outfit and assumed the role of Clark Kent, he was still Superman. He was awkward, had trouble communicating confidently with Lois Lane, and he never made a good Clark Kent. It was never who Superman truly was. The uniform or cape did not define Superman. The power that existed inside of him made him Superman.

Unfortunately, too few people think about themselves that way. They define who they are by their Clark Kent costumes—their job, car, house, the number of letters behind their name, their achievements or worse yet, their children's achievements. They believe society's view of who they are and think their identity comes from what they do or have, not who they are.

When working with high school athletes, we stress that their identity cannot be wrapped up in being an athlete. If their worth is defined solely by what they do on the athletic field or court, they are destined for a fall. Even for the most gifted athletes, the day will come when their playing days will end. Then what?

Many lawyers' identities are wrapped up in being a lawyer. It defines them and gives them value. However, those who derive their feelings of self-worth from practicing law often end up hollow and broken, repeatedly in divorces and with children who felt emotionally neglected.

A common adversity is the loss of a misplaced identity. The "big fish in the small pond" who moves to a big pond is just another fish. Here are some familiar examples: the high school homecoming queen who realizes she is more girl next door than cover model; the rising star at work who suffers a professional setback; and the spouse whose partner leaves.

The belief that our identity is defined and dependent on society is bogus. Your identity comes from who you truly are—the truth you know in your heart and soul—not who or what society says you are. It comes from who you are on the inside. It comes from God, who put greatness, love, and purpose inside you.

Focus on what you have and the treasures inside you. You have unique gifts and talents that belong only to you. Do not forget your superpowers. You have the tools to navigate the obstacles in your journey.

DECISION 11

DECIDE TO BUILD
RESILIENT HABITS

THIN THREADS AND SOLID CABLES

R esilient people take action. It is their most critical tool. Even more powerful are their repeated actions. Consistent, regular actions become habits and define who we become.

One guru of motivation is Dr. Robert Gilbert, the creator and host of Success Hotline (which will be discussed more later in this section). He has a saying that resonates:

Actions determine attitudes and attitudes determine moods.

The premise is true. Even when we do not feel like doing something, we can change the way we feel by taking action. When you stand straight and smile, you feel better than when you slump and frown.

Dr. Kelly McGonigal, a psychologist from Stanford University, wrote: "Put yourself in a happier position, and you can boost your mood. Practice a depressed face and slumped posture, and watch the gloom set in."[98] In a 2012 journal article, Dr. McGonigal described a study where participants were asked to perform two stressful tasks—one a mental challenge and the other a pain induction—while they held a chopstick with their mouths. Some participants were asked to hold the chopstick in a way that recruited the muscles of a genuine smile, some were asked to hold the chopstick in a way that recruited the muscles of a fake smile (mouth only), and others were asked to hold the chopstick in a way that did not mimic a smile at all.

The researchers measured the participants' heart rates and stress levels during and after the mental challenge and pain task. The finding? Those who were using the muscles required for a genuine smile were less stressed and showed faster physiological recovery from the stressful tasks than those mimicking a fake smile or those who did not smile.

The body has a direct connection to our mind. As Dr. McGonigal found: "Sitting up straight or standing tall improves self-confidence and mood; hugging yourself reduces pain; breathing slowly and deeply reduces stress and improves mood; leaning toward something (or someone) make (sic) you less anxious or afraid."[99]

The converse rarely works. We can rarely change the way we feel without first taking action. So, if you want to change how you feel, if you want to change your mood, begin to move. American psychologist Harry Stack Sullivan wrote: "It is easier to act yourself into a new way of feeling than to feel yourself into a new way of acting."[100]

One way to incorporate a take-action frequency into your lifestyle is to use the "fifteen-minute pledge"—a success mechanism I learned from Dr. Gilbert. It is premised on the truism that: "A body at rest tends to stay at rest, and a body in motion tends to stay in motion." If there is something you know you ought to do but resist doing it, agree with yourself to do it for just fifteen minutes. Don't want to work out, read, do that hard but critical task? Agree to do it for fifteen minutes. Often, once started, you will find you have momentum and can complete the task, even when it takes longer than fifteen minutes.

What Soil Are You Planted In?

Our lives become the sum-total of the things we do routinely, and those things shape who we are. Living a life of resilience involves being intentional about the things we do habitually. It means being intentional about the daily actions that shape our lives.

A flower cannot bloom if it is planted in poor or rocky soil. The soil makes it impossible for the flower to grow. In the same way, our daily habits and practices are the soil that fosters or stymies our growth. Resilient people have habits and practices they do daily that lead to success and fulfillment and away from failure. *How do you start a productive habit? What habits are productive?*

It Is the Start That Stops Most People

The prospect of being resilient can be a daunting mission. Early in the book, I shared the story of the donkey in the hole who got free by shaking off dirt and rising one step at a time. Sometimes, finding resilience means making small changes one step at a time. Small changes lead to bigger results and bigger changes. Eventually, you rise out of the momentary hole to freedom.

Rear Admiral William H. McRaven served as a Navy Seal. During a distinguished career, he served in many posts, including commander of the special operations. Admiral McRaven is credited with organizing and overseeing the execution of Operation Neptune Spear, the special operations raid that led to the death of Osama bin Laden on May 2, 2011.

Just before his retirement from active duty in June 2014, Admiral McRaven gave the commencement address at the University of Texas. In it, he shared his thoughts with the graduates on "How to Change the World." You might expect that Admiral McRaven, one of the great Navy commanders of our generation, would have some profound or deep principle of leadership as his first and most significant way to change the world. The advice he gave was profound only in its simplicity. His first piece of advice to change the world was . . . make your bed. After he explained that the first task each morning in SEAL training was making the bed perfectly, he shared this:

> *If you make your bed every morning you will have accomplished the first task of the day. It will give you a small sense of pride, and it will encourage you to do another task and another and another. By the end of the day, that one task completed will have turned into many tasks completed. Making your bed will also reinforce the fact that little things in life matter. If you can't do the little things right, you will never be able to do the big things right . . . So if you want to change the world, start off by making your bed.[101]*

In some ways, it is remarkable that one of our great military commanders would emphasize the importance of making the bed to graduates of one of the top schools in the country. However, in other ways, it emphasizes the importance of small things and the importance of getting started. These are the seeds that accomplish world-changing things.

Developing habits that foster resiliency starts the same way. The most important part of starting a resiliency-inducing habit is just that—starting.

I am a planner and enjoy planning what to do with details, timelines, and research. I can get so engaged in **planning** the action that I never **take** the action. Other times, the thought of starting something hard scares me away from starting at all.

The key to starting a habit can be found in one of the all-time great dad jokes: How do you eat an elephant? One bite at a time.

The same can be said for starting a habit. Do you want to lose forty pounds? Focus on losing the first two. Do you want to do something (or stop doing something) for the next forty days? Focus on one day, one hour, or one minute if you must.

Steve Hayes has successfully coached high school football in Texas and Oklahoma for thirty years. With his teams, he uses the term "One Minute Discipline." It is a reminder, especially when a player is fatigued, to focus on being disciplined in execution for the next minute. Then, focus on the next minute after that. The same is true with habits. Focus on executing the next step in the journey.

You may already have habits and practices you want to implement that will change the way you see yourself and will provide a productive soil for your resilience. If you are struggling to decide what habits and practices might make a difference for you, here are a few thoughts.

Great Habit #1: Attacking the Day with Purpose

A component of resilience is taking control of your day and being intentional about what you do. Build confidence that you are in control and will not yield that control to your feelings and emotions.

Be mindful of how your day starts. Before you allow news or messages from your phone into your consciousness, be intentional about doing these two things first: (1) engage in a practice that brings meaning to your life; and (2) make a plan for your day. Here are some ideas for practices that bring meaning to your life: identifying three things for which you are grateful, identifying two things that you can do to make the day great, reading the Bible or other inspirational texts, praying, meditating, exercising, or repeating affirmations. These are just ideas, and you may have others, but the concept is to be intentional about how you start the day. For someone struggling with an illness or physical handicap, a meaningful morning practice may be the reminder to stay positive. For someone overcoming addiction, a meaningful morning practice may be a reminder to stay clean and the consequences of not doing so, and an affirmation that you can win the day.

Then, after engaging in the meaningful morning practice, plan your day—what you are going to do and when. This simple act can take you off autopilot and allow you to be in control. Of course, things will pop up that can take you off-schedule. That is fine and expected, but why not start the day with a plan? Then, for important events in your day, spend a few moments visualizing how you want those events to go. There is more about visualization in the section about Decision 8. The morning planning time is a great time to identify the most meaningful events of the day and create a mind movie about how you want those events to play out.

For many years, Jim Cooper taught the seventh and eighth-grade boys bible class on Wednesday night at my Church. Jim was just gruff enough to keep order in a class of young teenage boys prone to disorder, but he was loving enough for us to know he cared. Mr. Cooper is one of those men who undoubtedly influenced thousands of lives by deeply pouring into hundreds of boys who came through his class and later became husbands, fathers, employers, and employees.

Mr. Cooper and I keep in touch via Facebook. He posts nuggets of wisdom. I asked his permission to share one that bears on starting the day with intentionality:

> *ADVICE: When you wake up each morning, and BEFORE you get out of bed, determine, in your mind (only takes 3 seconds) to MAKE it a GREAT day. Not a good day, not a nice day, BUT a GREAT day. The MAKE part infers you have a choice and the power to deal with whatever comes your way. MAKE this a habit, and settle this matter BEFORE your feet hit the floor each day. Let no one or no thing steal your joy. Guard it ferociously, all day, every day. This one habit has transformed my life. Jesus promised me a full and abundant life. He HAS delivered![102]*

Each morning, one of my habits on my drive into work is to listen to Dr. Gilbert's Success Hotline. Dr. Gilbert has recorded this free, three-minute message each morning since 1992 (which is remarkable!). It is the first thing I do when I get in the car. Dr. Gilbert is a professor of sports psychology at Montclair State University and covers a variety of topics about peak performance, mental toughness, and motivation in his messages. The podcast is available on Apple Podcasts. Search "Ironclad Success Hotline." Subscribe and listen. It is daily nutrition for your mind.

GREAT HABIT #2: DEVELOPING A RHYTHM OF GRATITUDE

Gratitude (and its close cousin, appreciation) is the intentional act of remembering and acknowledging good things in our lives. It is a way of looking at the world that makes the good things jump into the foreground. It spotlights the people in our lives who bring us joy. Gratitude applies a vibrant highlight to otherwise rarely noticed blessings, like clean streets, health, or food to eat. In the face of adversity, brokenness, and despair, gratitude has tremendous power to energize, make us resilient, provide healing, and bring hope.

However, is it counterintuitive to cultivate a habit of gratitude when things are going poorly, adversity has struck, and we are in the proverbial hole? While easy to feel grateful when things are going well, no one feels grateful to lose a job or a home, have a blow to their health, suffer a financial setback, or experience a trauma. It takes disciplined intentionality to find the positive in the hard things. *Amor Fati.* Making flame and brightness out of every circumstance we encounter.

There is a vital distinction between feeling grateful and expressing gratitude. We cannot easily will ourselves to feel grateful, less depressed, or happy. However, as discussed at the beginning of the section, feelings follow our actions. Expressing gratitude is a choice. When practiced, gratitude can become a prevailing mindset that endures and is relatively immune to the daily whims of our lives. When disaster strikes, gratitude provides a perspective from which we can view life in its entirety and not be overwhelmed by temporary circumstance. Expressing gratitude will affect the way we look at the world.

Gratitude is not magic. It cannot make problems and threats disappear. However, consciously cultivating a habit of gratitude builds a psychological immune system that can cushion us when we fall. There is scientific evidence that grateful people are more resilient to stress, whether minor everyday hassles or major personal upheavals.[103] Gratitude can also lead to better sleep, reductions of physical pain, a greater sense of well-being, and an improved ability to handle change.[104]

The German theologian and Lutheran pastor, Dietrich Bonhoeffer, was a staunch opponent of the German Nazi regime in the early 1940s. He was arrested in April 1943 and accused of association with the plot to assassinate Adolf Hitler. On Christmas Eve 1943, from Tegel prison, Bonhoeffer wrote a letter to his niece and to one of his students. In that letter, Bonhoeffer wrote: "gratitude converts the pangs of memory into a tranquil joy."[105] The meaning of his words took on added significance as a political prisoner in an authoritarian regime facing almost certain death.

In addition to the way gratitude changes how we feel, it also enhances our relationship with other people. Of course, as discussed in the section about Decision 4, connection with others is one of the primary tools of the resilient. It is intuitive that expressions of gratitude strengthen social bonds. However, it has also been research-tested.

We experience positive feelings when someone expresses gratitude or appreciation for who we are or something we have done. However, what effect does it have on the person who expresses the gratitude?

A team of researchers conducted a series of studies to answer that question. One study asked the participants to spend three weeks focusing on going the extra mile to express gratitude to a friend. This would include expressing gratitude both verbally and in writing beyond anything that they might normally do.[106]

The researchers found that the participants who completed the requested gratitude tasks experienced a marked increase in their perception of the strength of the relationship with their friends. This was likely derived from two factors. When we are intentional about finding things we like about someone, then our focus is on those positive attributes and it causes us to more fully value and appreciate the relationship. Additionally, when someone receives our gratitude and reciprocates it, the warmness of emotions further strengthens the relationship.

Another set of researchers studied impulses in the brain when expressing gratitude. They found that grateful brains showed enhanced activity in the areas that are associated with emotional processing, interpersonal bonding and rewarding social interactions, moral judgment, and the ability to understand the mental states of others. [107] One researcher, Glenn Fox, said: "The pattern of [brain] activity we see shows that gratitude is a complex social emotion that is really built around how others seek to benefit us."[108]

Another scientific expert on gratitude, Robert Emmons, sees a direct connection between gratitude and increasing social connection. "I see it as a relationship-strengthening emotion, because it requires us to see how we've been supported and affirmed by other people. . . . We recognize that the sources of this goodness are outside of ourselves. . . . We acknowledge that other people—or even higher powers, if you're of a spiritual mindset—gave us many gifts, big and small, to help us achieve the goodness in our lives."[109]

Emmons argues that gratitude, when practiced regularly, becomes a critical cognitive process—a way of thinking about the world that can help turn disaster into a stepping-stone. He argues that if we are willing and able to look, we can find a reason to feel grateful even to people who have caused us pain. We can thank that boyfriend for being brave enough to end a relationship that was not working, or we can thank the boss for forcing us to face new challenges. Perhaps we can even silently thank the traitorous friend for allowing us to value loyal relationships more deeply. This is yet another application of the E + R = O principle. An adverse **E**vent caused by one of our relationships can be transformed by a grateful **R**esponse that then creates an **O**utcome that propels us forward instead of pushing us back.

My wife sets the tone for practicing gratitude in our house. She has a large glass jar in the kitchen we call the gratitude jar. Next to the gratitude jar is a cup with pens and dozens of small slips of paper. Whenever we recognize something for which we should be thankful, we write it on a slip of paper and put it into the jar. Annually, we sit around the kitchen table, dump all the slips out, and read them one by one, remembering all the things that happened over the past year that we were thankful for. It is a powerful and emotional practice. We quickly forget so many great things that have happened. Reading through those slips is a wonderful reminder.

At the first annual reading, something unexpected happened. During the preceding year, we faced struggles or obstacles, got through them, and put a note of thanks about passing through the struggle in the gratitude jar. When reading through those slips of paper, it was striking how many issues that had seemed big and insurmountable, at the time, had been resolved and quickly forgotten. The annual review of the gratitude jar was a great reminder that hard times pass.

Another powerful gratitude practice is journaling. Although I have used different systems, I am a fan of the *Five Minute Journal* created by Alex Ikonn and UJ Ramdas. They describe the Journal as: "The simplest, most effective thing you can do every day to be happier." In the morning, spend a few minutes contemplating and writing about three big questions: *What am I grateful for? What would make today great? Who or what am I?* Then, in the evening, answer these two questions: *What are amazing things that happened today? What could I have done to make today even better?* Engaging in this practice of journaling does so many things to boost resiliency. It kickstarts the practice of gratitude in the morning, forces you to identify key things you can do to up-level your day, and creates a space to visualize how you want those key interactions to go. Then, it engages the power of affirmations (discussed more below) early in the day. Finally, at night, it again forces you to consider the things for which you are grateful. If you want an effective system to ingrain the act of gratitude, I highly recommend the *Five Minute Journal*.

A final gratitude practice is the long-lost art of the hand-written "Thank You" note. I endeavor to write and mail a note each workday to express gratitude to people who have done something I find admirable. Sometimes, I write to someone who has done something recently. Sometimes, I write to someone who helped me years ago. I try to be specific in my notes. The reason for this is simple: I think the expression of gratitude feels more authentic as it gets more specific. I want the recipient to know that I was genuinely paying attention, and this is not an empty ritual.

GREAT HABIT #3: DAILY AFFIRMATION

For a long time, I resisted the advice to use daily affirmations. It just seemed too hokey. However, once I considered all the negative messages that bombard me day after day after day, I got past my ego and engaged in the practice of reminding my mind who I want to be. The advertising industry spends incredible sums of money to learn the psychology behind getting us to buy products. They know from research that a critical first step in the formula is to create an emotional need, which they commonly deliver through a message that says we are not good enough or have lack. We hear and see these messages all around us on television, billboards, radio, in magazines, advertisements, and various messages each day that tell us there is something not right in our life that, of course, their product can fix.

> IT IS IMPERATIVE TO COUNTER THE MESSAGES OF "NOT GOOD ENOUGH" WITH AN INTENTIONAL AND REPEATED INTERNAL DIALOGUE ABOUT WHO WE ARE, OUR SUFFICIENCY, THE PERSON WE WANT TO BE, AND THE FUTURE WE WANT TO BUILD.

A Harvard study considered the effect of priming our brain, *i.e.,* delivering a specific message to ourselves. In the research, the staffs of seven hotels were studied and monitored. Half the participants learned their work was considered exercise. They were told how many calories they burned each day, and that their daily work satisfied the CDC's recommendations for an active lifestyle. The other half of the participants had the same jobs but received no priming information. Several weeks later, the group who had been told their work was exercise lost weight, lowered their blood pressure, and lowered their body fat. The other half, though doing the same jobs and moving the same amount, did not lose weight.[110]

The act of a daily affirmation builds this same belief in your mind. You will activate the Baader-Meinhof phenomenon (described in the section about Decision 8) to put your life into integrity with your affirmations. This is a long-term play, however. As Muhammad Ali said:

> *It's the repetition of affirmations that leads to belief. And once that belief becomes a deep conviction, things begin to happen.*[111]

As discussed in the section about Decision 8, Ali began to say, "I'm the greatest" before he became the heavyweight champion. However, his affirmation led to the reality. We can look with the benefit of hindsight and lose track of the significance of Ali's belief in himself. Ali becoming a champion was a long shot.

He hated working out. He said: "I hated training, but I said: *'Don't quit. Suffer now, and live the rest of your life as a champion.'*"[112] Ali's vision of himself and his affirmation about what his future would hold drove him past the point of discomfort to engage in workouts he hated. He had this kind of drive to make his reality match his affirmation.

* * *

Mark DeJesus is an author, public speaker, teacher, and former radio host. Mark is gifted in helping people address the core issues that become limitations to their God-given identity and destiny. He has become a friend and confidant. Mark has a routine affirmation practice. I asked him to share his thoughts on it with me. This is what he said:

Daily affirmations became a lifesaver for my emotional and spiritual health. It helped me out of some of the toughest seasons of my life, especially because it taught me how to have a better relationship with myself, to love myself and allow God's love to empower me into overcoming.

Personally, I started off simple. Every man has his moment in the mirror, getting himself ready. So while brushing my teeth, shaving and getting ready for the day, I would look at myself in the mirror and speak words of encouragement and love. It felt weird at first and there was resistance inside to this. But I found there to be such healing and strength as I stuck with it. Looking at myself in the eyes while saying it had an interesting power to it.

My words were often simple: "God, you love me. I love myself. I have what it takes to overcome today." Then the list grew, because I began to love the habit. When you enjoy a habit, it's easy to return to it.[113]

USING LEVERS

Once a productive habit is identified, the next step is ingraining it into a daily practice. Stated differently, to change the soil we are planted in, we must ingrain our habits into something we do routinely.

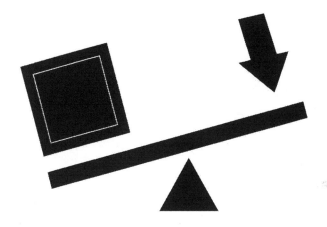

A lever is relatively simple technology. The function of the lever is to reduce the amount of required force to move an object. To do so, a lever increases the distance through which the required force acts. For instance, a one-pound force with the benefit of a lever can move more than one pound. The lever multiplies the amount of movement that results from the applied force.

When enacting change in our lives, we also have natural internal levers. Our motivations and actions are governed by the forces of pain and pleasure. Avoiding pain or experiencing pleasure pushes us in one direction or the other. As we get in touch with and understand these forces, they have tremendous leverage over our actions. If you have identified an unfulfilled core value, try connecting to your pain and pleasure forces to materialize that value in your life.

The more emotional the connection to the pleasure/pain levers, the stronger they are. Think about what you have identified as "don't want," then internalize the reasons you don't want that. Think about what you do want and the benefits that will accrue if you obtain what it is you do want.

So, for example, if you have a core value of being physically fit but are struggling to exercise or have the discipline to eat well, then write the benefits you will achieve from reaching your fitness goal. Maybe you will have more energy, will feel more confident in your body, and will eliminate health risks or limitations. But also, write the things you give up if you do not reach your fitness goal. Maybe you will experience health problems and will have to take costly medication. Maybe you are setting an example for your kids that you do not like.

> WE ARE WHAT WE REPEATEDLY DO. EXCELLENCE, THEN, IS NOT AN ACT BUT A HABIT . . . —WILL DURANT (1926)[114]

Think about what you do want—your goal, your Outcome. In your mind, fully step into and feel the benefits you will get. Visualize and magnify the benefits by enhancing any mental images, experiencing the sensations, tastes, sounds, or scents. *How will you feel? What will people say? What will it be like to walk down the street?* Find that feeling in your body and spin it faster and faster, feeling it deeply.

Then, really visualize the fear and pain of failing to reach your objective. Magnify the feelings by making the images more vivid, the sensations more real; try to hear associated sounds and experience any related smells or odors.

Maybe a pleasure lever is buying a new pair of jeans when you hit a milestone on the scale. Better yet, buy the jeans and hang them up where you can see them but do not allow yourself to wear them until you make your milestone. That has both a pleasure and pain lever. Other pain levers might include no visits to a favorite restaurant until a goal is reached, giving $100 to a friend (or, if you want to increase the intensity, an enemy) if you miss a goal, or giving up your favorite beverage until a goal is reached. Tony Robbins tells the story of a lady who decided to eat a can of dog food if she did not make a milestone weight by a date certain. She set the can out on the kitchen counter as a reminder. That's hardcore!

MAKE SMALL CHANGES; ONE HABIT AT A TIME

When trying to enact change in your life, focus on making small changes—one habit at a time. Trying to change too many things at once will lead to failure across the board.

Research has shown you are two to three times more likely to experience success with a new habit if you make a specific plan for when, where, and how you will perform the changed behavior. Psychologists call these specific plans "implementation intentions." An implementation intention might look like this: I plan to work out five times a week. This week, I will work out at my gym at 7:00 a.m. on Monday, Tuesday, Thursday, and Friday and will take a three-mile walk on Saturday morning. Developing a specific plan for when, where, and how you will make a habit of a new action will dramatically increase the odds that you will follow through, especially if you focus on one thing at a time.[115]

Ingraining a new habit requires significant conscious effort to remember to do it. You must enlist your prefrontal cortex—the thinking part of your brain—and apply conscious effort, intention, and thought. Then, after performing the new routine enough times for connections to be made and strengthened in your brain, the behavior will require less effort as it becomes the default pattern.[116] The pattern of behavior then becomes a normal routine and eventually becomes mindless and automatic. This process is called automaticity, the ability to perform a behavior without thinking about each step so that the pattern is automatic and habitual. In sports, we call it muscle memory. Automaticity occurs as the result of repetition and practice. As more and more repetitions accumulate, a behavior becomes more automatic. This is part of the reason the first twenty or so days of a new habit are crucial. In the beginning, automaticity is low. After twenty days, the habit becomes more routine. There is some tipping point at which new habits become automatic. The time it takes to build a habit depends on many factors, including how difficult the habit is, what your environment is like, your genetics, and more.

It took me many years, and many failures, to internalize that the best way to make positive change is by not trying to fix everything at once. Instead, it is best to focus on one specific habit, work on it until you master it, and make it an automatic part of your daily life. Then, repeat the process for the next habit, and so on, and so on.

A new habit will begin as a thin thread that is easily broken. You may forget it or let it slip and have to resume the activity. However, as you make the habit automatic, the habit and the actions that make up the habit become a strong cable not easily broken.

Then, delving even a level deeper, when you first try to incorporate a new habit, learning how to do it is fragile. Like the thin thread, your process can easily break. However, as you become more adept at implementing life-changing habits, one-by-one your process for ingraining habits becomes stronger, and you become more confident in it. In fact, your process for implementing life change, *i.e.*, habits, becomes a strong cable of its own. You start the life change with confidence that you know how to implement it successfully.

Consistent, regular actions that transform into habits define who we become. To start your way out of any hole, begin with your daily actions, your daily habits. Small ones, done one at a time. Maybe begin with making your bed.

DECISION 12
DECIDE TO FORGIVE AND RELEASE RESENTMENT

THE FIELD OF EMPTY CHAIRS

I walked through a field of empty chairs. It was sobering to see the 149 large and 19 small chairs in rows. Monumental twin bronze gates stand on both sides of the space.

The time of 9:01 on the eastern gate represents the last moments of peace for the Alfred Murrah Federal Building in Oklahoma City. On the opposite end, the western gate reads 9:03 and represents the first moments of recovery.

The chairs in the field are hand-crafted from glass, bronze, and stone and represent those who lost their lives in the bombing that happened at the Murrah Building at 9:02 a.m. on April 19, 1995. Each chair has a name etched in the glass base.

The field of chairs sits where the Murrah Building once stood. The chairs are arranged in nine rows to symbolize the nine floors of the building. Each person's chair is on the row representing the floor where the person worked or was located when the bomb went off. The chairs are also grouped according to the blast pattern. There are more chairs where the building was most heavily damaged, and the five chairs on the outside represent five people who died from the blast but were not in the building.

The nineteen smaller chairs represent the children killed in the bombing. It was hard to take my eyes off the smaller chairs as I imagined what their parents must have felt that day.

There is an elm tree on the north side of the field of chairs. Before the bombing, this was the only shade tree in the parking lot across the street from the Murrah Building. The people who worked in the building used to arrive early to get one of the shady parking spots provided by its branches. From historic photos taken in the 1920s, the tree was estimated to be a century old on the day of the bombing. The old elm tree was taken for granted prior to the blast. Heavily damaged by the bomb, the tree survived after nearly being chopped down during the initial investigation when workers wanted to recover evidence hanging in its branches and embedded in its bark.

The force of the blast ripped most of the branches from the tree. Glass and debris were embedded in its trunk, and fire from the cars parked beneath it blackened what was left. Most thought the tree could not survive.

* * *

One name on the chairs is Julie Welch. Julie was twenty-three. She lived in Oklahoma City and was working as a Spanish interpreter for the Social Security Administration. Her office was in the Murrah Building.

Julie's goal was to be a teacher. She had recently graduated with a degree in Spanish from Marquette University in Milwaukee, Wisconsin, and was on the dean's honor list. In high school, she spent a year as a foreign exchange student in Pontevedra, Spain. During college, she returned to Spain for a year and attended Marquette en Madrid. Julie felt strong compassion for those less fortunate than herself. She frequently visited Little Flower Church in a poor region of Oklahoma City where many Hispanic families resided, and she spoke with the children to pass along a ray of hope for their future. Julie's hope was to marry a lieutenant she met at the nearby Tinker Air Force Base. When the bomb went off, Julie's dream shattered, much like the building around her. Julie was in her office assisting two Spanish-speaking men at 9:02. Julie and the two men were all killed.

* * *

On the morning of April 19ᵗʰ, Bud Welch was getting ready for his shift at the Texaco garage. As he often did, he was going to meet Julie, his only daughter, for lunch later that day. However, his morning was shattered when his entire home shook. Bud's brother phoned. He was in his car listening to the radio and saw plumes of smoke in downtown Oklahoma City. The local news suspected there had been an explosion at the courthouse. Welch turned on the TV as a traffic helicopter zoomed in to a familiar-looking building. "My God, it's not the courthouse. It's the Murrah building." Bud's thoughts immediately turned to Julie.[117]

In an interview given twenty years after the event, Bud recounted: "You could see that on the north side of the building there was nothing there. It was just gone. I pretty much gave up all hope then. She was killed on the Wednesday morning. Her body was found on the Saturday. I knew. If she'd been alive the first thing she would have done was call her dad."[118]

"From the moment I learned it was a bomb," Bud remembers, "I survived on hate."[119] His anger was focused on the two men responsible for the bombing, Timothy McVeigh and Terry Nichols. Like so many others, Bud wished for their speedy conviction and execution.

In speeches given after the event, Bud told audiences: "The year after Julie died was the most miserable I've ever been in my life."[120] Bud admitted to the crowds he began self-medicating with alcohol and went through a long period of wanting retribution. He visited the bomb site every day after Julie's death.[121]

Nine months after the event, Bud experienced a turning point in his journey on one of his daily trips to the bomb site. Bud spotted the old elm tree. Julie routinely parked her car near that tree. Despite its scars from the blast, the tree had survived and had sprouted new branches. "The thought that came to me then seemed to have nothing to do with new life," he recounted. "It was the sudden, certain knowledge that McVeigh's execution would not end my pain."[122]

Bud was watching the people across the street leave things at the memorial. Crosses, rosaries, silk flowers. Bud said, "Every muscle in my body ached from alcohol poisoning. I said to myself: 'You are not moving forward. What you are doing is not working.' "[123]

Another turning point for Bud was meeting Timothy McVeigh's family. It started with seeing McVeigh's father on television. Bud felt an emotional shift that day: *"Oh, dear God, I thought, this man has lost a child too."*[124] In September 1998, over three years after the bombing, Bud was going to be in Buffalo, McVeigh's hometown. Bud decided it was time to meet Timothy's father.

Bud's initial impression of Bill McVeigh was that he was a "regular Joe," just like Bud. He also met Bill's daughter, Jennifer, who reminded Bud of Julie's friends. "I know what happened to me that Saturday morning in western New York is that I met a bigger victim of the Oklahoma City bombing than myself," said Welch.[125]

Bud described the first meeting as "an emotional one." He remembered: "When we finished talking, Jennifer got up and walked around the table and she grabbed me around the neck and started hugging me. We can't change the past," Bud told Bill and Jennifer, "but we have a choice about the future."[126]

On June 11, 2001, Timothy McVeigh was put to death. Bill said, "There was nothing about that process that brought me any peace."[127]

The old elm tree that started Bud on his road to recovery and forgiveness is now called the Survivor Tree. It still stands as strong as ever. Hundreds of seeds from the Survivor Tree are planted annually, and the resulting saplings are distributed each year on the anniversary of the bombing. Thousands of Survivor Trees are growing in public and private places all over the United States.[128]

* * *

One of the primary barriers to resiliency is resentment. In *Notes of a Native Son*, James Baldwin, one of the voices of the civil rights movement, wrote: "I imagine one of the reasons people cling to their hates so stubbornly is because they sense, once hate is gone, they will be forced to deal with pain."[129]

Forgiveness is ultimately for the benefit of the forgiver, not the person being forgiven. When we carry resentment or when we see ourselves as a victim, we carry a heavy burden that keeps us from getting past an obstacle. Forgiveness allows us to put the burden down and walk away from it.

Bud Welch will never forget his daughter, Julie, or the events of April 19, 1995, in Oklahoma City. He may never escape the loss in his heart. However, until he released the anger and resentment he harbored against the bombers, until his heart changed toward them, he could not move ahead. He had to move past self-medicating and, as James Baldwin said, "toward dealing with the pain."

Without forgiveness, we are constantly stuck in our past. Some people spend years of their lives in bitterness and resentment when they could—through forgiveness—have spent the time recovering and rediscovering joy and peace.

Sometimes we are affected by big, earth-shattering events, like the loss of a loved one through someone else's actions—whether intentional or accidental. Maybe someone has hurt us in a way that makes it very hard or impossible to heal. However, sometimes we also get hung up on relatively minor things.

The Masked Bandit of Resentment

In a classroom full of students, a professor asks: "If you had $86,400 and someone stole $10 from you, would you spend the rest of your money trying to track them down for revenge?"

The students all agree they would let it go. The professor then says: "There are 86,400 seconds in a day, and time is much more valuable than money. You can always work for more money, but once a second passes, you can never get it back. Every time someone upsets us, it probably took around 10 seconds, so why do we throw away the other 86,390 seconds worrying about it or being upset." The professor concluded: "We all make this mistake. It is time to start letting things go."

Resentment is like a bandit that steals from us. It steals time, joy, and our ability to be resilient and move past the obstacles in front of us. Resentment is like a masked bandit because we rarely recognize we have given our resentment the power to keep stealing from us.

In 2012-2013, twenty banks in the City of Dallas and its surrounding suburbs were robbed by a perpetrator the FBI dubbed the "Mesh-Mask Bandit." The bandit entered the bank with a black mesh mask covering his entire face. It allowed him to see but disguised his identity to anyone who saw him.

For months, images of the robber were shown on television and on electronic billboards from a police drawing the FBI had composed with the help of an eyewitness who saw the bandit before he pulled on his mask and entered a bank. Despite being a high priority for the FBI and local law enforcement, the robber remained free, and hits on the banks continued. The robberies sometimes came a week or two apart. Sometimes they were more frequent. On February 20–21, 2013, the Mesh-Mask Bandit robbed three banks in two days. They were within a two-mile radius of each other.

One evening in the summer of 2013, my wife approached me with her cell phone. She showed me a picture of our next-door neighbor.

"Isn't this our neighbor?"

I recognized him and had talked to him in his yard a few times and even went inside his home on one occasion to take him mail that had been inadvertently delivered to our house. He and his wife were normal neighbors with adult kids who visited them from time to time. They kept up with their yard. They had two dogs. He had started a Spanish-speaking television station and was often interviewed on issues affecting the Latino community. We saw them at local restaurants and said hello.

"Yes, why?" I said.

"Read the story."

I did and was flabbergasted. Our neighbor had just been apprehended by the FBI and was being charged as the Mesh-Mask Bandit. I had only paid token attention to the story up to that point. Now, I read with rapt attention. Our *normal* next-door neighbor was a bank robber and one of the most prolific bank robbers I could ever remember—twenty banks. The next day, news trucks and police cars lined our street. News reporters shot interviews against the backdrop of the bandit's seemingly normal house.

Have you allowed the masked bandit of resentment to live next to you? Without ever realizing it, our resentment can continue to steal from us for months or years when masked as the original wrong done *to you,* like the bomber who took your daughter, the drunk driver who took your son, the boss who took your job, the charlatan who took your opportunity. However, when we allow resentment to control us, the original perpetrator no longer steals from us. It is a new, masked perpetrator we allow to continue to steal from us. However, we can also release the resentment and forgive.

THE NATURE OF FORGIVENESS

Some are slow to forgive—or never forgive—because they feel they cannot excuse the wrongful conduct of another. However, forgiving does not mean you condone wrongdoing. Reaching a place of true forgiveness is not deciding what someone did is acceptable if it was not.

Forgiving does not mean you have to forget (is that even possible?). Rather, forgiveness is eliminating the negativity that results from hurt by releasing the emotional baggage. It is retaining control over the bandit stealing more and more from you.

Before Bud Welch could become resilient, he had to forgive the men who killed Julie. He did not condone or forget what they did. However, he chose to keep living much like the old elm tree, the Survivor Tree.

The Survivor Tree witnessed incredible tragedy. It took pieces of shrapnel, was cut and gashed, and its leaves—the main sign of its life—were ripped and torn. Still, it kept living.

The cuts and gashes in the old tree eventually healed, and its leaves returned. The Survivor Tree still bears the scars of the damage done to it. Those scars, like memories, will forever be present. Yet it still lives, and its seeds spread throughout the country, creating life and new trees in places where they did not exist before.

Like that old elm tree, forgiveness allows scars to heal, leaves to regrow, and new seeds to be spread. One key to resiliency—to becoming a Survivor Tree in your life—is to forgive and move forward.

Here's to you continuing to spread seeds of life.

Decision 13
DECIDE TO ABSORB THE WISDOM OF THE STRUGGLE

Giving Yourself to the Mountain

We love the underdog story, the big comeback, winning against all odds. During the NCAA Basketball Tournament (often called March Madness), we root for the lower seed to surprise the higher seed. Movie producers give us stories like Cinderella because we pay to watch them. We want David to defeat Goliath.

Intrinsically, we know the biggest challenges produce the greatest stories of victory, faith, and perseverance. Each adversity we face can be a stepping-stone. Early in the book, the donkey that fell in the well used the dirt being shoveled on him as steps to his ultimate rescue and freedom. The same can be true for us. The dirt shoveled on us—the adversities, obstacles, failures—can be transformed into stepping-stones if we learn from and absorb the lessons from the adversity.

In difficult situations, the lessons are more insightful and more deeply ingrained than the daily occurrences. Lessons learned in adversity have the potential to change, in a significant way, how you think and live, the way you see yourself, and your future results. Many great startup success stories have an adversity as their catalyst. Adversity can often be the push needed to compel action.

Bill Gates and Paul Allen's first business venture was called Traf-O-Data, a service created to read data from roadway traffic counters that could be compiled into reports for traffic engineers. The business experienced only modest results. However, twenty years later Paul Allen said, "Even though Traf-O-Data wasn't a roaring success, it was seminal in preparing us to make Microsoft's first product a couple of years later."[130]

Walt Disney's first effort to produce cartoons was a Kansas City-based company called *Laugh-O-Grams*. It filed bankruptcy shortly after it started.[131] However, Disney learned from the experience, moved to Hollywood, and started what became Walt Disney Studios.[132]

Milton Hershey started in the candy business by setting up a candy shop in Philadelphia. After five years, the business failed. Hershey next tried making candy in Chicago. He was not successful. Then, he tried New York. Again, he failed. After ten years of disappointment, Hershey started the Lancaster Caramel Company. This one started to work. He eventually sold the company to get the money to start the Hershey Chocolate Company.[133] Today, everyone knows about Microsoft, Walt Disney, and Hershey chocolate. However, these revolutionary businesses would not exist without their founders' ability to learn from their failures and start again.

When adversity strikes, there are things to be learned. There are insights to be gleaned. To find the wisdom in the struggles we encounter, here are four questions to consider.

1. What did I learn from this?
2. What can I do better?
3. Do I have a bad habit that contributed to this?
4. Are there other adversities like this one that might happen that I can plan for or avoid?

Not all these questions are applicable to every adversity, but one or two of the questions—when answered with brutal honesty—can yield deep and valuable insight. The goal is not to relive the experience but to get a deeper perspective from it. Emotional venting without accompanying insight does not produce change. No amount of reflection about the event will help until and unless you are able to take a fresh, redemptive perspective on it.

ADVERSITY AS A CATALYST TO JUMPSTART CHANGE

The dead battery. I have had my share of times when I have gone out to the car, turned the key, and nothing happened. On the dashboard, the battery light was illuminated in red. So, I pulled out the jumper cables and started looking for a Good Samaritan to help me jumpstart my car. The jumpstart is a surge of energy delivered from the working car into the dead one that carries enough charge to allow the car to start and recharge itself.

Adversity can have the same effect. It is a forced way for you to refocus, a pattern interruption in your normal day-to-day habits and routines. Those habits and routines may result in lacking energy, drive, or a charge—like a dead battery. Your habits and routines may have taken you down a path you do not want to travel. The adversity can help you find a surge of energy sufficient to reboot your normal routines.

Use this interruption to think about the adversity and its cause and to re-examine what matters to you. If, during this time, you discover what matters to you the most has been neglected, then you have received a great lesson and can rectify that going forward. If you are neglecting your core values, then you will not have an optimal feeling of fulfillment.

You are on this planet for a reason. Adversity can help you rediscover purpose and take charge of your life. Assuming you take this lesson from adversity, you will no longer wake up late, be uninspired, or show up with less than your best self. Your purposes and core values are too important to settle for less.

THE BARKLEY MARATHONS

There is something life-giving about being pushed to the edge—or perhaps past the edge—of where you thought your limits were. This explains the ultimate endurance event known as the Barkley Marathons. For the first two decades of its existence, almost no one knew about the event unless they had competed in it or knew someone who did. However, a series of blog posts and articles culminated in *The Barkley Marathons: The Race That Eats Its Young*, a 2015 feature-length documentary about the race. The event's founder is Gary "Laz" Cantrell. To picture Laz, imagine Duck Dynasty crossed with a retired marathon runner. Laz is a long-bearded, potbellied, cigarette-smoking mountain man. He is accompanied on a race weekend by his pit-bull, Big. (His other dog, Little, apparently stays home). Laz was a lifelong marathoner and ultramarathoner in the days before ultramarathoning was a thing. Laz and his wife, Sandra, live in a farmhouse in Bell Buckle, Tennessee, a town an hour south of Nashville with a population of a little over 500.

The race is fittingly held on the Saturday closest to April Fool's Day. While there are other ultra-marathons, trail runs, long-distance hikes, Tough Mudders, obstacle races, and other tough-guy endurance contests, the Barkley is unique among them. The Barkley is generally considered the most difficult endurance event in the world by almost any measurement. It comprises a 100-mile trek—five loops, approximately twenty miles each—up and down the mountains in Frozen Head State Park, about an hour northwest of Knoxville, Tennessee. Most of the race is off-trail.

Competitors get a twelve-hour time limit to complete each of the five loops. While twenty or so miles in twelve hours would seem doable to the uninitiated, the Barkley course is not so simple. "Sometimes it's like climbing the side of the Grand Canyon," says ultrarunner Charlie Engle, who entered the 2010 race, "through briars and thick brush." He adds: "And you're having to navigate to small points far away to the tops of ridges. If you go to the wrong ridge, you're screwed."[134] In 2006, a computer scientist named Dan Baglione got lost on loop one and stumbled all the way into the next county before finding his way back to the start thirty-two hours later.[135]

The Barkley course has no direction or trail markings. Competitors are only allowed to take a map, a compass, their instinct, and their experience to navigate the trail. Getting off-track and taking wrong turns are common and add time and mental fatigue to an already challenging event. "It wears on you to get lost," says Stu Gleman, a retired academic who lives in Franklin, North Carolina and has run the Barkley multiple times. "And everybody gets lost a little bit."[136]

During the race, competitors face thorny bramble bushes and vines, unpredictable early spring weather, sleep deprivation, and a cumulative climb equal to twice the height of Mount Everest. The course records at other prestigious 100-mile races are around 15 hours.[137] The best finish time at Barkley is fifty-two hours and three minutes. Complete one loop in under twelve hours, and you are allowed to head out on your second loop, and then your third, fourth and fifth, if you are still within the time limits and willing and able to continue. The first Barkley Marathon was held in 1986. Through its first thirty-three years, only 15 people have finished the full distance.[138] Many competitors never finish the first loop.

The 2019 race took place on March 30. The start time, known only to Cantrell, varies from year-to-year and is not disclosed to the participants until one hour prior to the start. In 2019, the race started at 8:23 a.m. The weather on the first day was sunny with a high of eighty degrees. Later in the day, a cold front blew in, bringing freezing rain that turned to sleet at the base of the course and snow at the top.[139]

Forty runners started the race. Only twenty-eight finished the first loop. Twenty-two runners started loop two. Only seven finished. Only six started loop three. Only two started loop four. No one started the final loop.[140]

The Barkley is more, however, than just an extreme physical test. Gleman, who has been running ultramarathons for twenty years, talks about the Barkley and its participants in spiritual, reverent tones. He says:

> *The thing is, they're compulsive overachievers and they've found something that convinces them they're still alive and doing something . . .* **Everybody here has seen the big sadness—even the young people have figured life out, and they're looking for something to convince themselves that they're real and they're accomplishing something.** *And the race is sort of like that, too. They're all very sensitive, very human people. The main thing is, it's not masochistic in the slightest. These people aren't into pain and misery and laceration and all that. They're into accomplishing something, matching themselves against a huge thing, even if it's just a joke, and taking it as far as they can . . . One of the mistakes first-timers make is to try to conquer the mountain. That ends badly. What I tell people—and anybody who's done it, even the big dogs will tell you this—is to just give yourself over to it.*[141]

Laz Cantrell, known more for sardonic descriptions of the misery of the Barkley, will offer an occasional glimpse into why he keeps hosting the event. "It's inspiring," Cantrell says. "This is an incredibly hard thing, and they're trying to do it."[142]

There is something to the thought of not trying to conquer the mountain but to giving yourself over to it. When we see adversity as a phase and an arena of life to lean into, experience, and learn something about ourselves, it is far easier to avoid the negative emotions of shame, resentment, and self-pity and keep our eyes and spirit open to what the adversity teaches us. We become richer in life experience and more robust and resilient as we navigate obstacles and glean the lessons from them. There is something inspiring in tackling a hard thing; something self-revealing in the struggle. Do not miss the wisdom of the adversity that you have walked, are walking, or will walk through.

And once the storm is over, you won't remember how you made it through, how you managed to survive. You won't even be sure whether the storm is really over. But, one thing is certain. When you come out of the storm, you won't be the same person who walked in. That's what this storm's all about. —Haruki Murakami, Kafka on the Shore (2002)[143]

DECISION 14
DECIDE TO PREPARE THE CHILD FOR THE PATH

A WORD FOR PARENTS

In March 2019, news broke about several high-profile families that federal prosecutors alleged were part of a scheme to improperly influence admissions decisions at several top-tier universities. The families were accused of paying more than $25 million to a "college admissions consultant" who used the money to fake student test scores and bribe college officials to secure admission for the families' children.

The leader of the fraud, the so-called college admissions consultant, William Rick Singer, entered a plea bargain and then helped the Federal Bureau of Investigation (FBI) gather incriminating evidence against the families. Singer admitted to fraudulently securing college admission for over 750 families. The FBI's investigation was named Operation Varsity Blues.

Singer had two schemes. The first involved cheating on the SAT or ACT college admission exams, standardized tests used by colleges both to determine admission and to award merit-based scholarships to top students. Singer found psychologists who, for a fee of several thousand dollars, completed false paperwork used to certify clients' children as having a learning disability. Once certified, the students received accommodations, such as extra time to complete the standardized tests. The same sham reports were also used to obtain testing accommodations during the students' enrollment in college, giving the students an unfair advantage over their peers.[144]

Singer also had improper influence at two testing centers, one in Los Angeles, California and another in Houston, Texas, where stand-in test takers posed as the student in question and took the test under the student's name. Mark Riddell, a Harvard alumnus and preparation director at IMG Academy for college admission exams, pled guilty to being one of the stand-in test takers. He was reported to have received as much as $10,000 per test.[145]

The second scheme used by Singer was even more sinister. Using a charitable foundation, Singer funneled money to college athletics staff and coaches to help get a student admitted into a college for which they would not otherwise qualify. Program coaches or athletic staff identified the student as a potential athlete to the admissions office, even if there was no intention of the student joining the sports program. Students recruited for admission slots set aside for athletic teams have substantially higher admission prospects than other students.

In one such incident, the former men's tennis coach at the University of Texas was accused of accepting approximately $60,000 in exchange for designating an applicant as a recruit for the Texas Longhorns tennis team, thus facilitating their admittance into the university.[146] The government alleged a similar fraud at Yale where the then head coach of the women's soccer team was said to have falsely identified an applicant as a recruit for $450,000.[147] A former senior associate athletic director and water polo coach at USC allegedly received $1.3 million and $250,000, respectively, for similar schemes.[148] There were comparable allegations made against programs at Stanford, UCLA, Wake Forest, Georgetown, the University of San Diego, and other schools.[149]

PREPARING THE CHILD FOR THE PATH

Many were aghast that parents would go to these lengths and spend this kind of money to get their child into a prestigious university. However, Operation Varsity Blues is just one symptom of a larger issue—parents who prepare the path for the child instead of preparing the child for the path.

Speaking from experience, it is hard to see your child fail. It hurts on an emotional level to see someone you love hurting.

We can also take it as a commentary on our value as parents. When our child fails, we can easily slip into viewing ourselves as failures as parents. It is another version of keeping up with the Joneses. Jimmy Jones (made-up name) down the street is on the honor roll, playing in the most competitive youth sports program, and excelling in piano recitals. If our child is making B's, is a backup on the recreational sports team, and is far more into video games than playing classical music, we can view ourselves as inferior.

We must learn to disconnect our worth as parents from our children's performance. Obviously, we should strive to parent our children to the best of our ability. This may even include actively learning how to be a better parent. However, while we can control how we parent, we do not have total control over what or how our children do. This is yet another arena where we must control the controllables and not obsess over the things we cannot control.

Just as we encourage our athletes to release themselves from tying up their worth with the outcome of a contest because things out of their control will influence it, we must do the same as a parent. Our children ultimately have a substantial say in how they are or what they do. As parents, we must accept that and stop basing our sense of worth on how our children turn out. If we parent the best we can, we must turn over the reins to our child and to God.

The wise parent does not fix every pothole or detour in the child's path. The experience of failure or hardship is necessary for the child's growth. Being a great parent does not mean a child is perfect or that their path is perfect.

FILLING IN THE GAPS

I carry anxiety about how I parent my three boys. I feel an obligation to teach them all the things they need to know to be successful in life, work, relationships, and spirituality. However, as they hit their teen years and had less interest in hearing what I had to say, it became increasingly apparent that I could never teach them everything. I might not even be able to teach them the major things, or even all the important things. As I get older (and perhaps wiser), I am becoming increasingly aware that I do not have sufficient grasp of all those things myself, much less am I in a position to teach them all.

Someone wise told me that our job as parents is to do the best we can and then it is up to God to "fill in the gaps." As an imperfect parent with imperfect kids, that brought me peace.

This comes full circle to where the book started. If we ought to expect a life where adversity arises, where we continue to learn into our adulthood, where obstacles are a part of our growing experience, then we cannot reasonably expect our children will learn everything they need when under our roof, nor would we want them to. At the end of the day, we are preparing the child to navigate her or his path.

LAW SCHOOL—AN EXPERIENCE IN LEARNING HOW TO THINK

Law school is largely an exercise in learning how to prepare the future lawyer to navigate the path. I entered law school with the mistaken notion I would spend three years learning the intricacies of the law. During the three years, sometimes that occurred. However, most students graduate from law school knowing only a small percentage of actual law.

A far more important activity happens in law school. The first year is largely spent learning how to think and solve legal problems, including how to find applicable law. It is the law school version of preparing the student for the path. Law schools call it "learning how to think like a lawyer."

Learning how to think about the law and solve a legal problem includes identifying the issues that need to be resolved or answered. Issue-spotting—as it is called—is one of the most critical skills of a good lawyer. Even if the lawyer does not know the answer to every question, they can identify the question and find the answer.

This is quite practical, as you consider it. Laws, rulings, and society change. The ability to see a problem, spot issues, and then know where to go to find the answers to those issues ensures the lawyer is equipped to address his or her clients' needs even as times bring change.

This is an apt analogy for parenting. I may not be able to pre-program wisdom into my children to address every issue they may have. However, if I can teach essential skills for success—resilience, an appreciation for continual learning, compassion, empathy, humility, joy, hope, faith—then they can apply those skill sets to whatever life throws at them. It is the law school equivalent of learning how to think. It is a mindset of being able to find success, even during a failure or adversity.

When children are equipped with a mindset that lets them navigate the obstacles of life themselves, it becomes unnecessary (and unwise) to clear their path. Or to buy their way into a top university.

WISDOM FROM A SOUTH TEXAS LAWYER

David Patton has been one of the most accomplished lawyers in the oil and gas industry in Texas over the last forty years. He has helped clients with some of the biggest deals in the industry. Deservedly, he is highly trusted. However, his wisdom extends beyond the fields of law or the oil and gas industries.

I was fortunate to be his law partner for almost twenty years, and David routinely sent out words of wisdom he had learned from growing up in a hard-working family in the Rio Grande Valley in South Texas. South Texas is a hard place with rough summers, arduous labor, and dangerous terrain. David gleaned learnings from his childhood and related them to holidays or world events.

Recently, David penned a letter to his adult children that he later shared on Facebook. It had tremendous wisdom, and with David's permission, I share it here:

Letter to My Adult Children With Children:

Although I did not appreciate it at the time, one of the best and longest lasting gifts my Rio Grande Valley parents gave me was the expectation that I contribute to the family enterprise by performing assigned chores. There were both daily tasks and more unique ones that came along from time to time. It was made clear that these were my personal responsibility and they had priority over any other activity, especially play time.

Every morning I was expected to make my bed and clean my room. I was to take my dishes to the sink and rinse them, sometimes washing and drying. It was my job to take out the trash.

In addition to regular chores, on weekends and summer days, my mother would leave me a list on the kitchen table of special tasks for the day. I could not leave the house before they were done. If I hustled, it usually took 2-3 hours to complete them. Sometimes it would be vacuuming, dusting or mopping. I hung washed laundry on the clothesline. Weeding was my least favorite, but at least I was outside. Pasting Gold Stamps in gift books was a frequent task.

As I grew older my assignments included mowing the yard and trimming. My hands grew calloused from shovels and hoes. I was used as an errand boy, first on my bike and later in the car. I learned to paint along side my mother. I did carpentry with my dad (never very well). These were not optional.

My parents were smart to impose time constraints. Not just prioritizing the chores over fun, but setting real time deadlines. If it had to be done by noon when my mom came home from college, I couldn't sleep all morning.

They did me another favor. When a chance to get a paying job came along, they not only encouraged me, they expressed appreciation that I was adding to family resources. My mom and dad shared their experiences of hardship my extended family had experienced during the depression and WWII. But it was done with a spirit of gratefulness for their blessings.

One final gift. It was drummed into me that no matter the task, no matter how much I did not want to do it, it was to be done to the best of my ability. If others were involved, I was to contribute my share and never be out worked. The reward was not how much I was paid, but that I had done my best. That was reward in itself, leading to self-esteem not dependent upon the view of others or their relative success.

In the years since, my life has prospered when I followed the creed learned as a child. Many of my childhood friends also faced similar expectations that made them strong and independent.

I implore you to prepare your children by providing them with the discipline of responsibility. Give them small things to do, make sure that they do them and praise them for their effort. Have them join you in household matters. Expose them to what it takes to run a home. Expect much but only within their personal talents. As a parent, you are more than a chauffeur to activities, you are a sculptor of character that will mold your children's future.[150]

Well said, David. I hope we all glean wisdom from your parents.

CONCLUSION

In ancient times, a king had a boulder placed on a roadway. He then hid a short distance from the road to see if anyone would remove the huge rock. Some of the wealthiest merchants and aristocrats in the kingdom came down the road and walked *around* the boulder. Many loudly blamed the king for not keeping the roads clear, but none did anything to get the stone out of the way.

Then, a peasant came down the road carrying a load of vegetables. Upon approaching the boulder, the peasant set down his load and tried to move the stone to the side of the road. After much pushing and straining, he finally succeeded.

As the peasant picked up his load of vegetables, he noticed a purse lying in the road where the boulder had been. The purse contained many gold coins and a note from the king that said: "This treasure is for the person who removes the obstacle from the path."

The peasant experienced what too many never comprehend. Every obstacle presents an opportunity to gain treasure. It might be a financial reward, such as the gold coins in this parable. However, it might be a learning experience to enrich our lives or knowledge that we can navigate adversity to make us mentally tougher for the next challenge. It might be the wisdom that comes when we realize that the times of greatest growth come when we are pushing boulders out of our path.

My hope for each reader of this book is to walk away with a greater understanding of adversity, resiliency, and the tools to conquer the next adversity. Keep pushing. You have a second wind coming to carry you through. There is a reward when the boulder moves.

THANK YOU FOR READING!

Dear Reader,

My fervent prayer is that the message of *Second Wind* arrives in the heart and spirit of the people for whom it was intended. I hope there was a principle or thought that will help you through your current or next adversity. If you found the content worthy, please mention it to a friend or on social media. My account on Twitter is @J_Clint. Let me know if something in the book helped you.

While you are considering what you read, it would mean the world to me if you left an honest review on Amazon. As you know, reviews play an integral part in building relevancy for all products. They are also a great help to authors. Whether you loved the book or hated it, I would appreciate your feedback and your candid review will help others make an informed purchase.

Wishing you much success!

J. Clint Schumacher

ABOUT THE AUTHOR

Clint Schumacher is a husband, father, lawyer, and football coach. He is passionate about building teams that are resilient, engaged, and motivated. He has the unique experience of both working to solve complex legal problems and coaching young athletes to succeed. He has studied, applied, and taught the principles of resilience set out in this book. They work. He has helped clients obtain over $100 million in judgments or settlements. He has completed a marathon, climbed the Sydney Harbour Bridge, delivered two TEDx talks, won a bellyflop contest, and finished deep in the money at the World Series of Poker. He holds a Bachelor of Business Administration from Abilene Christian University in Accounting and a Juris Doctorate from the University of Texas at Austin. You can find more of his work at www.jclintschumacher.com.

ENDNOTES

1. Lucius Annaeus Seneca, *Moral Letters to Lucilius: Letters from a Stoic – Volume 1*, trans. Richard M. Gummere (Toronto: Aegitas 2015), Letter I, 7, Google Books.

2. Jeffrey Gitomer, "You are the Essence of Your Reactions and Your Responses," accessed December 11, 2020, https://www.gitomer.com/you-are-the-essence-of-your-reactions-and-your-responses/#.

3. This idea is often credited as a quotation by Thomas Edison; however, the author could not find any original writings where Edison said or wrote those words. Another quote that is credited to Edison in response to the statement that it was a shame he had spent so much time working on an invention without getting results: "No results? Why, man, I have gotten a lot of results! I know several thousand things that won't work." This was recorded in the 1915 biography *Thomas Alva Edison* written by Francis Rolt-Wheeler.

4. James Bennett, "Mandela, at White House, Says World Backs Clinton," *New York Times,* September 23, 1998, https://www.nytimes.com/1998/09/23/us/testing-president-visitor-mandela-white-house-says-world-backs-clinton.html. Though Mandela uttered the quote in 1998, it is originally credited to Oliver Goldsmith in his book from 1762: *The Citizen of the World: or, Letters from a Chinese Philosopher, Residing in London, to His Friends in the East.*

5. *Webster's Ninth New Collegiate Dictionary* (Springfield, MA: Merriam-Webster, 1988), s.v. "Self-pity."

6. Marcus Aurelius, *Meditations,* trans. Gregory Hays (New York: The Modern Library 2002), Book 10, p. 140, Kindle.

7. Thomas Szasz, *Anti-Freud: Karl Kraus's Criticism of Psychoanalysis and Psychiatry* (Syracuse, NY: Syracuse University Press, 1990), 81, Google Books.

8. Maria Konnikova, *The Biggest Bluff: How I Learned to Pay Attention, Master Myself, and Win*, Read by Maria Konnikova (New York: Penguin Audio 2020), Chapter 6, "No Bad Beats," Audiobook.

[9] Susie Moore, "What Sara Blakely Wished She Knew in Her 20s," *Marie Claire*, November 4, 2014, https://www.marieclaire.com/politics/news/a11508/sara-blakely-interview/.

[10] Glenn Mangurian, "Realizing What You're Made Of," *Harvard Business Review* (March 2007), https://hbr.org/2007/03/realizing-what-youre-made-of.

[11] Jack Canfield and Janet Switzer, *Success Principles: How to Get From Where You Are to Where You Want to Be* (New York: William Morrow 2015), Principle 1, Google Books.

[12] Ryan Speedo Green, "Ryan Speedo Green: From juvenile delinquency to opera stardom," interview by Scott Pelley, *60 Minutes*, CBS, June 16, 2019, https://www.cbsnews.com/news/ryan-speedo-green-from-juvenile-delinquency-to-opera-stardom-60-minutes-2019-06-16/.

[13] Green, interview.

[14] Green, interview.

[15] Anthony Tommasini, "Young Talents Working With Those Comedians Stravinsky and Berlioz," *New York Times*, February 12, 2014, https://www.nytimes.com/2014/02/13/arts/music/evening-of-comic-opera-from-the-met-and-juilliard.html.

[16] In 2016, Green's life was the subject of the book *Sing For Your Life: A Story of Race, Music, and Family* by Daniel Bergner. To listen to Mr. Green, there are several videos available on YouTube. His performance in the Hollywood Bowl with the Los Angeles Philharmonic Orchestra can be found here: https://www.youtube.com/watch?v=7iFyqp0nt9c.

[17] *Wikipedia, The Free Encyclopedia*, s.v. "Second wind," (accessed September 12, 2020), https://en.wikipedia.org/wiki/Second_wind.

[18] William Wilkerson, "Dumas is a 'No Excuse' Zone Thanks to Dedication of Antonio Murga." *Dave Campbell's Texas Football*, June 10, 2020, http://www.texasfootball.com/article/2020/06/10/dumas-is-a-no-excuse-zone-thanks-to-dedication-of-antonio-murga.

[19] Lance Lahnert, "Dumas Team, Community Rally Behind Assistant Facing Stage 4 Cancer," *Amarillo Globe-News*, August 7, 2018, www.amarillo.com/sports/20180807/dumas-team-community-rally-behind-assistant-facing-stage-4-cancer.

[20] Wilkerson, "Dumas is a 'No Excuse Zone.'"

[21] *Ibid.*

[22] *Ibid.*

[23] *Ibid*

[24] Antonio "Coach's" Obituary, Retrieved December 5, 2020 from https://www.morrisonfuneraldirectors.com/obituary/antonio-coach-murga.

[25] Brené Brown, "Shame v. Guilt," *Brené Brown* (January 14, 2013), https://brenebrown.com/blog/2013/01/14/shame-v-guilt/#:~:text=I%20

define%20shame%20as%20the,makes%20us%20unworthy%20of %20connection.

[26] Gen. 2:25 (New International Version).

[27] Gen. 3:8 (New International Version).

[28] Jerry Wyckoff and Barbara C. Unell, *Getting Your Child from No to Yes: Without Nagging, Bribing, or Threatening* (Minnesota: Meadowbrook Press, 2004), 47.

[29] Brené Brown, "Shame Resilience Theory: A Grounded Theory Study on Women and Shame," *Families in Society: The Journal of Contemporary Social Services* 87(1) (2006): 43-52, https://doi:10. 1606/1044-3894.3483.

[30] Ecclesiastes 1:9 (NIV).

[31] Taylor Conroy, "Reinventing rock bottom," filmed September 20, 2017 at TEDxRoyalRoadsU Conference, Victoria, British Columbia, video, https://youtu.be/6lEC3W4YpQ4.

[32] Theodore Roosevelt, "Citizenship in a Republic," Speech at the University of Paris, April 23, 1910. The full text of the speech can be found here: https://www.leadershipnow.com/tr-citizenship.html.

[33] Roosevelt, speech.

[34] Roosevelt, speech.

[35] Jenny Mulks, "Hold on to hope," filmed March 1, 2019 at TEDxFlowerMound, Flower Mound, Texas, video, https://youtu.be/ dMaK4j62I9s.

[36] Jenny Mulks, in discussion with the author, July 2020.

[37] Mulks, discussion.

[38] Mulks, discussion.

[39] Jeremy Merchant and Tami Merchant, in discussion with the author, July 2020.

[40] "Boxing: Buster Douglas Reveals the Pain Behind Knocking Out Mike Tyson," *New Zealand Herald*, (December 24, 2018), https://www. nzherald.co.nz/sport/news/article.cfm?c_id=4&objectid=12182125.

[41] Jon Margolis, "It's Tyson in Just 93 Seconds," *Chicago Tribune*, July 23, 1989, https://www.chicagotribune.com/news/ct-xpm-1989-07-23-8902200515-story.html.

[42] The HBO broadcast of the fight is available on YouTube here: https:// youtu.be/XLsgIuswYdY.

[43] Jonathan Snowden, "25 Years After the Fall: Mike Tyson, Buster Douglas and Boxing's Biggest Upset," *Bleacher Report*, February 11, 2015, https://bleacherreport.com/articles/2358930-25-years-after-the-fall-mike-tyson-buster-douglas-and-boxings-biggest-upset.

[44] Kelley D. Evans, "Buster Douglas: I Wasn't Impressed With the Success Mike Tyson Was Having," *The Undefeated*, December 11,

2018, https://theundefeated.com/features/buster-douglas-i-wasnt-impressed-with-the-success-mike-tyson-was-having/.

[45] HBO Broadcast.

[46] Mark Podolski, "It's Been 25 Years Since Buster Douglas Knocked Out Mike Tyson," *Willoughby News-Herald*, February 10, 2015, https://www.news-herald.com/sports/mark-podolski-its-been-25-years-since-buster-douglas-knocked-out-mike-tyson/article_d7c17425-7353-5cce-8ab0-cd66b9175fea.html.

[47] Evans, "Buster Douglas Reveals."

[48] Richard Cunningham, "Sail the Right Ships," LinkedIn, January 30, 2019, https://www.linkedin.com/pulse/sail-right-ships-richard-cunningham/.

[49] Kalhan Rosenblatt, "Desiree Linden, first U.S. woman to win Boston Marathon in 33 years, is 'on cloud nine,'" *NBC News*, April 17, 2018, https://www.nbcnews.com/storyline/boston-bombing-anniversary/desiree-linden-first-u-s-woman-win-boston-marathon-33-n866571.

[50] *Wikipedia, The Free Encyclopedia*, s.v. "Desiree Linden," (accessed June 13, 2020), https://en.m.wikipedia.org/wiki/Desiree_Linden.

[51] Jennifer Calfas, "Boston Marathon Winner on How She Nearly Quit – and Why She Slowed Down for Her Competitor's Bathroom Break," *Time*, April 17, 2018, https://time.com/5242871/boston-marathon-winner-desiree-linden-almost-quit/.

[52] Desiree Linden (@des_linden), Twitter, April 16, 2018, https://twitter.com/des_linden/status/985966360785276928?lang=en.

[53] Calfas, "Boston Marathon Winner."

[54] Germaine Gaspard, "The Power of Using Your Pain to Fuel Your Success," filmed March 1, 2019 at TEDxFlowerMound, Flower Mound, Texas, video, https://youtu.be/SJ2KArlkSZc.

[55] "Life after Losing a Child," *DFW Child*, November 2012, https://dfwchild.com/life-after-losing-a-child/.

[56] "Life after Losing."

[57] This is often credited with being a story arising from Taoist philosophy in China.

[58] William B. Irvine, *A Guide to the Good Life: The Ancient Art of Stoic Joy* (New York: Oxford Press 2009), 10, Google Books.

[59] Oliver Burkeman, *The Antidote: Happiness for People Who Can't Stand Positive Thinking* (New York: Farrar, Straus and Giroux 2012), 29.

[60] *Encyclopedia Britannica*, s.v. "Five Good Emperors," accessed April 25, 2020, https://www.britannica.com/topic/Five-Good-Emperors.

[61] Ronald Mellor, *The Historians of Ancient Rome: An Anthology of the Major Writings*, 3rd ed. (New York: Routledge 2013), 518, Google Books.

[62] Aurelius, *Meditations,* Book 4, p. 38 (3).

[63] Aurelius, *Meditations,* Book 4, p. 47 (49a.)

[64] Aurelius, *Meditations,* Book 3, p. 31 (9).

[65] Epictetus, *The Enchiridion,* trans. Elizabeth Carter (The Internet Classics Archive), http://classics.mit.edu/Epictetus/epicench.1b.txt

[66] The Eastern Washington University study appears to have first been reported in Robert Emmons' book, *Gratitude Works!*

[67] Robert Emmons, "How Gratitude Can Help You Through Hard Times," *Greater Good Magazine,* May 13, 2013, https://greatergood.berkeley.edu/article/item/how_gratitude_can_help_you_through_hard_times.

[68] Gal. 1:13-14 (NIV).

[69] 2 Cor. 11:24-27 (NIV).

[70] Acts 21:27-30 (NIV).

[71] Phil. 1:12-13 (NIV).

[72] Phil. 4:8 (NIV).

[73] Phil. 4:12-13 (NIV).

[74] Rom. 5:3-5 (NIV).

[75] Hugh S. Fullerton, "It's the Old Confidence That Wins Games," *The Pittsburg Press,* June 16, 1914, p. 23, Column 4 (Google News Archive).

[76] Elon Musk, "Joe Rogan Experience #1470," interview by Joe Rogan, *Joe Rogan Experience,* May 7, 2020, video 28:58, https://www.youtube.com/watch?v=RcYjXbSJBN8.

[77] Daniel Kahneman, *Thinking, Fast and Slow* (New York: Farrar, Straus and Giroux, 2011), 127-28, Google Books.

[78] Muhammad Ali (@MuhammadAli), Twitter, July 29, 2012, https://twitter.com/MuhammadAli/status/229606493916372992.

[79] Jere Longman, "In a Rout and a Romp, U.S. Takes World Cup," *The New York Times,* July 5, 2015, www.nytimes.com/2015/07/06/sports/soccer/womens-world-cup-usa-defeats-japan-to-win-title.html?ref=sports.

[80] Jim Carrey, interview by Oprah Winfrey, *The Oprah Winfrey Show,* February 17, 1997, www.oprah.com/oprahs-lifeclass/what-oprah-learned-from-jim-carrey-video.

[81] Avery Stone, "Kerri Walsh Jennings Says No Pressure for Rio Olympics," *USA Today,* February 23, 2015, www.usatoday.com/story/sports/olympics/2015/02/23/kerri-walsh-jennings-april-ross-rio-olympics/23913015/.

[82] Arnold Schwarzenegger and Douglas Kent Hall, *Arnold: The Education of a Bodybuilder* (New York: Simon & Schuster Paperbacks), 17-19, Google Books.

83 Steve Chandler, 100 Ways to Motivate Yourself, 3rd ed. (United States: Career Press, Incorporated, 2012), Chapter 2, "Stay Hungry," Google Books.

84 Tim Layden, "Ready to Rock," *Sports Illustrated,* February 17, 2010, www.si.com/more-sports/2010/02/17/vonn.

85 *Ibid.*

86 Seneca, *Moral Letters to Lucilius,* Letter VII, p. 18.

87 Tracy Kornet, "A Simple Message on One Man's Door Is Inspiring Thousands," *News 4 Nashville,* December 3, 2018, https://www.wsmv.com/news/a-simple-message-on-one-man-s-door-is-inspiring/article_d9bcb4ae-f783-11e8-be4b-33110bf61b8f.html.

88 Patrick Mead (@TravelingMead), Twitter, November 28, 2018, https://twitter.com/travelingmead/status/1067929429366792192?lang=en.

89 "Don English Does It Again," HS Baseball Web, May 14, 2009, https://community.hsbaseballweb.com/topic/don-english-does-it-again?page=1.

90 Don English, interview with author.

91 *Ibid.*

92 Napoleon Hill, *Think and Grow Rich* (New York: Start Publishing 2013), 267, Google Books

93 Michael P. Carey and Andrew D. Forsyth, "Teaching Tip Sheet: Self-Efficacy," *American Psychological Association,* 2009, https://www.apa.org/pi/aids/resources/education/self-efficacy.

94 "'Recycled Orchestra' Turns Trash into Music," *CBN News,* April 16, 2015, https://www1.cbn.com/cbnnews/world/2015/April/Recycled-Orchestra-Turns-Trash-in-Music.

95 *Ibid.*

96 *Ibid.*

97 *Ibid.*

98 Kelly McGonigal, Ph.D., "Smile Your Way Out of Stress?", *Psychology Today,* August 1, 2012, www.psychologytoday.com/us/blog/the-science-willpower/201208/smile-your-way-out-stress.

99 McGonigal, "Smile."

100 Douglas A. Bernstein, Bethany A. Teachman, Bumni O. Olatunji, and Scott O. Lilinfeld, *Introduction to Clinical Psychology,* 9th ed., (New York: Cambridge University Press 2020), 267 (*citing* Harry Stack Sullivan), Google Books.

101 Admiral William H. McRaven, "University of Texas at Austin 2014 Commencement Address," filmed May 19, 2014 at Austin, Texas, video, youtu.be/pxBQLFLei70.

102 Jim Cooper, Facebook Post, July 17, 2019, https://www.facebook.com/jim.cooper.524/posts/2925985040750605.

[103] Emmons, "How Gratitude Can Help You Through Hard Times."

[104] *Ibid.*

[105] Dietrich Bonhoeffer, "To Renate and Eberhard Bethge, Christmas Eve 1943," *Letters and Papers from Prison,* ed. Eberhard Bethge (New York: Touchstone, 1997), 189, Google Books.

[106] Nathaniel M. Lambert, Margaret S. Clark, Jared Durtschi, Frank D. Fincham, Steven M. Graham, "Benefits of Expressing Gratitude: Expressing Gratitude to a Partner Changes One's View of the Relationship," *Psychological Science* 21, no. 4 (March 5, 2010): 574–80.

[107] Glenn R. Fox, Jonas Kaplan, Hanna Damasio, and Antonio Damasio, "Neural Correlates of Gratitude," *Frontiers in Psychology* 6 (September 20, 2015), https://doi.org/10.3389/fpsyg.2015.01491.

[108] Adam Hoffman, "What Does a Grateful Brain Look Like?," *Greater Good Magazine,* November 16, 2015, https://greatergood.berkeley.edu/article/item/what_does_a_grateful_brain_look_like.

[109] Robert Emmons, "Why Gratitude Is Good," *Greater Good Magazine,* November 10, 2010, https://greatergood.berkeley.edu/article/item/why_gratitude_is_good.

[110] Alia J. Crum and Ellen J. Langer, "Mind-Set Matters; Exercise and the Placebo Effect," *Psychological Science* 18, no. 2 (February 2007): 165-71.

[111] Muhammad Ali (@MuhammadAli), Twitter, July 29, 2012, https://twitter.com/muhammadali/status/229606493916372992?lang=en.

[112] This quote appeared on Ali's Twitter account posthumously on May 15, 2017. The quote is attributed to Ali in many other places, including this article: Joyce Chen, "Muhammad Ali Dead at 74: 10 of the Boxing Legend's Greatest Quotes," *Us Weekly,* June 4, 2016, https://www.usmagazine.com/celebrity-news/news/muhammad-ali-dead-at-74-10-of-his-greatest-quotes-w208811/.

[113] Mark DeJesus, interview with author.

[114] Will Durant, *The Story of Philosophy* (New York: Pocket Books, 2006), 98, Google Books.

[115] Amy Dalton and Stephen Spiller, "Too Much of a Good Thing: The Benefits of Implementation Intentions Depend on the Number of Goals," *Journal of Consumer Research* 39, no. 3 (October 2012): 600-14.

[116] Debbie Hampton, "The Neuroscience of Changing Your Behavior," *The Best Brain Possible,* January 8, 2017, https://thebestbrainpossible.com/the-neuroscience-of-changing-your-behavior.

[117] Fran Singh, "How an Oklahoma Bombing Victim's Dad Made Friends with Timothy McVeigh's Father," *The Guardian,* April 18,

2015, https://www.theguardian.com/us-news/2015/apr/18/oklahoma-bombing-victim-father-friends-tim-mcveigh-dad.

[118] Singh, *How an Oklahoma Bombing.*

[119] Bud Welch, "Losing His Daughter in the Oklahoma City Bombing Transformed Him," *Guideposts*, May 1999, https://www.guideposts.org/better-living/life-advice/coping-with-grief/losing-his-daughter-in-the-oklahoma-city-bombing-transformed-him.

[120] Singh, "How an Oklahoma Bombing."

[121] Singh.

[122] Welch, "Losing His Daughter."

[123] Singh, "How an Oklahoma Bombing."

[124] Welch, "Losing His Daughter."

[125] Singh, "How an Oklahoma Bombing."

[126] Welch, "Losing His Daughter."

[127] Singh, "How an Oklahoma Bombing."

[128] "The Survivor Tree – Tomorrow," Oklahoma City National Memorial Museum, accessed September 13, 2020, https://memorialmuseum.com/experience/the-survivor-tree/the-survivor-tree-tomorrow/.

[129] James Baldwin, *Notes of a Native Son* (Boston: Beacon Press, 1955), 101, Google Books.

[130] Brent Schlender and Henry Goldblatt, "Bill Gates and Paul Allen Talk," *Fortune Magazine,* October 2, 1995, archive.fortune.com/magazines/fortune/fortune_archive/1995/10/02/206528/index.htm.

[131] *Biography*, s.v. "Walt Disney," April 27, 2017, https://www.biography.com/business-figure/walt-disney.

[132] *Biography*, Walt Disney.

[133] *Biography,* s.v. "Milton Hershey," April 27, 2017, https://www.biography.com/business-figure/milton-hershey.

[134] Lisa Jhung, "The Impervious Barkley Marathons," *Runner's World,* April 6, 2010, https://www.runnersworld.com/trail-running/a20802738/the-impervious-barkley-marathons/.

[135] Dave Seminara, "Few Know How to Enter, Fewer Finish," *New York Times,* March 27, 2013, https://www.nytimes.com/2013/03/28/sports/the-barkley-marathons-few-know-how-to-enter-fewer-finish.html.

[136] Matthew Everett, "The Barkley Marathons is the Toughest Race You've Never Heard Of, *Metro Pulse*, April 13, 2011, https://web.archive.org/web/20110825100319/http://www.metropulse.com/news/2011/apr/13/barkley-marathons-toughest-race-youve-never-heard/.

[137] Matthew Everett, "A Record-Setting Weekend at the Barkley Marathon, the Race That Eats Its Young," *Knoxville Mercury*, April

6, 2016, https://www.knoxmercury.com/2016/04/06/record-setting-weekend-barkley-marathons-race-eats-young/.

[138] "Barkley Marathon Finish Stats," *Cactus to Clouds,* October 9, 2018, https://cactustoclouds.com/2018/10/09/barkley-marathons-finishers/.

[139] Andrew Dawson, "Once Again, No Participants Were Able to Finish the Barkley Marathons," *Runner's World,* April 1, 2019, https://www.runnersworld.com/news/a27003724/no-finishers-barkley-marathons/.

[140] Dawson, "Once Again."

[141] Everett, "The Barkley Marathons" (emphasis added).

[142] Everett, The Barkley Marathons.

[143] Haruki Murakami, *Kafka on the Shore,* trans. Philip Gabriel (New York: Alfred A. Knopf, 2005), 5-6, Google Books.

[144] Information filed by the U.S. Government in Cause No. 19-CR-10078, *United States of America v. William Rick Singer,* in the U.S. District Court for the District of Massachusetts, available at: www.justice.gov/file/1142901/download.

[145] Information filed by the U.S. Government in Cause No. 19-CR-10074, *United States of America v. Mark Riddell,* in the U.S. District Court for the District of Massachusetts, available at: www.justice.gov/file/1142891/download; *see also* "College Admissions Scandal: Who Is Mark Riddell, the 'Smart Guy' Who Took Tests for Kids?" *NBC New York,* June 10, 2019, www.nbcnewyork.com/news/national-international/college-admissions-scandal-who-is-mark-riddell-took-tests-for-kids/1645895/.

[146] Information filed by the U.S. Government in Cause No. 19-CR-10116, *United States of America v. Michael Center,* in the U.S. District Court for the District of Massachusetts, available at: www.justice.gov/usao-ma/page/file/1152581/download.

[147] Information filed by the U.S. Government in Cause No. 19-CR-10075, *United States of America v. Rudolph Meredith,* in the U.S. District Court for the District of Massachusetts, available at: www.justice.gov/file/1142886/download.

[148] J. Brady McCollough, "USC Fires Administrator and Coach Arrested in College Admissions Fraud Scheme," *The Morning Call,* March 12, 2019, www.mcall.com/la-sp-college-admission-scam-coaches-usc-20190312-story.html.

[149] Affidavit of Laura Smith, available at: www.justice.gov/file/1142876/download.

[150] David Patton, "Letter to My Adult Children with Children," Facebook, April 3, 2019, https://www.facebook.com/david.patton.5602/posts/2581175191895157.

Made in the USA
Middletown, DE
12 May 2021

39540796R00097